F

FINANCING FARMER

COOPERATIVES

FINANCING FARMER COOPERATIVES

- NEEDS
- SOURCES
- POLICIES
- PROCEDURES and
- PROBLEMS

RUSSELL C. ENGBERG

Published by the Banks for Cooperatives 1965

Foreword

In 1962 the banks for cooperatives contracted with Dr. Russell C. Engberg to make a comprehensive study of procedures and problems in financing farmer cooperatives in the United States, including particularly the policies and operations of the banks for cooperatives. The principal objectives were to develop suggestions for strengthening and improving the services of the banks and to explore possibilities for facilitating the financing of farmer cooperatives generally. The study was organized and carried out in close collaboration with the undersigned Planning and Advisory Committee. Plans and general results were also reviewed by a ten-member Consulting Committee composed of representatives from the Federal Farm Credit Board, district Farm Credit boards, and the board of directors of the Central Bank for Cooperatives. That study was completed and final reports were made to the banks in 1964.

The presidents of the banks believed that some of the material collected and a number of the ideas developed would be helpful to farmer cooperative officers and directors and to others interested in cooperative development. They felt also that there was a real need for a comprehensive publication on the financing of farmer cooperatives and that the study would provide an excellent foundation for it. Accordingly, Dr. Engberg was commissioned by the banks to carry out this assignment. His presentation, *Financing Farmer Cooperatives,* is made available in the belief that it will be a constructive addition to the literature on this subject.

Dr. Engberg was eminently qualified for the undertaking. He is a graduate of Iowa State University and holds an M.S. degree from the University of Minnesota and a Ph.D. from Columbia University. His experience includes five years of teaching, research, and extension work in agricultural economics; two years on the research staff of The Brookings Institution, Washington, D. C.; and assignments as a consultant in agricultural finance to European and Latin American nations in connection with technical cooperation programs of the United States government. He served in various capacities in the cooperative Farm Credit System for thirty-four years, including six and one-half years as director of research for the Farm Credit Banks of Omaha. When he retired in 1962 he was chief of the Research and Information Division of the Farm Credit Administration in Washington, a responsibility he had held for seventeen years.

As long as a supply is available, copies of this book may be obtained from any of the banks for cooperatives. The names and addresses of the banks are given at the end of the book.

Planning and Advisory Committee for Study of Trends in Financing Farmer Cooperatives:

Richard B. Jones, Jr., *President, Baltimore Bank for Cooperatives*

Lloyd L. Ullyot, *President, St. Paul Bank for Cooperatives*

Lindsay A. Crawford, *President, Berkeley Bank for Cooperatives*

Lester L. Arnold, *Chief, Research and Information Division, Farm Credit Administration*

Glenn E. Heitz, *Deputy Governor and Director of Cooperative Bank Service, Farm Credit Administration—Chairman*

Preface

The special study made for the banks for cooperatives in 1962-64 provided a great deal of the material used in this volume. To a considerable extent, it also furnished the reason for preparing a follow-up publication for wider distribution. A few comments about the initial assignment therefore may be appropriate.

The objectives of that study have already been stated in the Foreword. There were two major sources of information. One, of course, was the banks for cooperatives and the extensive accumulation of loan experience data in their files. The banks assisted freely in supplying loan case histories and other information, the preparation of which represented several man-years of work by bank personnel. This material was invaluable, and I am deeply indebted to all those who helped assemble it.

The other major source of information was interviews with cooperative leaders and workers. These included the following:

	Number
Managers and active officers of farmer cooperatives	55
Farmer-directors of cooperatives	19
Officers or directors of national cooperative organizations	7
Officers of state cooperative councils	6
Agricultural economists (colleges and Farmer Cooperative Service, USDA)	26
State departments of agriculture	2
Former presidents of banks for cooperatives	2
Officers of other agricultural organizations	2
Total	119

The purpose of the interviews was to confer with people who were informed about problems in financing farmer cooperatives and were in a position to give constructive ideas and suggestions. They represented a wide variety of operations and cooperative experience. They were also well distributed geographically, and the visits took me into literally every part of the United States. Since it was important to get "grass-roots" opinions, their views, freely expressed, constituted a very important source of information and ideas. These visits were an extremely rich experience, and the interested cooperation of those interviewed is gratefully acknowledged. I also valued my contacts with officers and employees of the Federal Land Banks and Federal Intermediate Credit Banks concerning the financing of farmer cooperatives.

Available published material bearing on the subject was examined. This included publications of colleges and universities, the Farmer Cooperative Service of the United States Department of Agriculture, the American Institute of Cooperation, and other cooperative organizations. Literature in the field of corporation finance was reviewed. The Farm Credit Administration cooperated in furnishing information and other services, with special help coming from the Cooperative Bank Service, the Research and Information Division, and the Accounting and Budget Division.

I am particularly obligated to the members of the Planning and Advisory Committee for their guidance and encouragement and for their patient reading of many long manuscripts. This indebtedness applies to both the original study and the preparation of this book.

Although the committee, the banks for cooperatives, personnel in the Farm Credit Administration, and others provided valuable guidance, ideas, and encouragement, they are not responsible for—nor necessarily in agreement with—the opinions or conclusions, either expressed or implied, in this book. Those which have been included are my sole responsibility.

RUSSELL C. ENGBERG

Contents

ix

Chapter ONE

Trends In Cooperative Development and Financing Implications

Since early Colonial days, farmers in the United States have worked together because they found that many things can be done better cooperatively than by individual action. At first such cooperation was informal, but beginning with a Michigan law in 1865, state governments have provided for incorporation of associations of farmers organized on cooperative principles. In their subsequent development and growth as incorporated businesses, farmer cooperatives have experienced most of the operating and management problems of other types of business concerns and generally have followed similar practices and principles in handling them.

Among the major requirements for success in virtually every business are adequate capital and effective financial management. Farmer cooperatives are no exception to this rule. In the early history of cooperative development, financing was one of the most difficult problems to be overcome. A large number of failures resulted from inadequate capital and unsound financing practices. While tremendous progress has been made in improving facilities and management, financing still presents one of the most critical areas of decision-making for organizers of farmer cooperatives and for the management and boards of directors of operating associations. Although some cooperative leaders believe that present sources

1

of capital and credit are still inadequate, the more frequently expressed view is that the real problem is financial management.

The objective of this volume is to examine in some detail the financing needs, facilities, practices, and related problems of farmer cooperatives in the United States. In addition to descriptions of financing arrangements and trends, this examination will include evaluations of some of the criticisms which have been made of certain financing facilities and policies and, where appropriate, suggestions for changes or improvements which might be constructive.

As stated in the Foreword and Preface, much of the material and many of the ideas developed during the special study made for the banks for cooperatives will be used in this discussion, including frequent references to the opinions and views of cooperative leaders and workers who were interviewed as part of that study. Numerous other sources have been examined and have provided significant data. Information regarding individual cooperatives which has been included to illustrate points being made has been obtained from published material or has been used with the permission of the cooperative concerned.

General Status of Farmer Cooperatives

Logical beginning steps in studying the financing of farmer cooperatives are to refresh one's mind regarding the nature of the organizations to be dealt with, to note briefly the manner in which they have developed, and to observe in somewhat greater detail the main characteristics of the recent and probable future growth trends. Such a review will permit a better understanding of the amounts and types of capital needed and of the related financing problems.

Considering first the distinctive features of the type of corporation with which this study is concerned, there are three fundamental principles that distinguish farmer cooperatives from other businesses. These are:

1. Democratic control by members. In a cooperative, control is associated with those who use and also own the business. It is common practice to limit each member to one vote, regardless of the amount of equity interest held or the amount of patronage. In a non-cooperative business corporation, voting control is associated with the amount of stock held.

2. Payment for capital limited to a conservative rate. In a cooperative, members make investments and assume related risk but are limited to only a fair rate of return (or none at all) on the investment. In a non-cooperative business, investors in stock assume the risk but also receive the profits after expenses are paid.

3. Sharing the benefits and savings in proportion to the patronage of the individual member. Any profits or net income after paying expenses, including a fair rate for the use of capital, belong to the members. They share in such benefits and savings in proportion to the amount of patronage rather than in proportion to the amount of their investment.[1]

Every state in the Union has a provision for incorporating farmer cooperatives, and although these statutes are not uniform, the basic principles outlined above are generally recognized. They are recognized also in a number of Federal statutes which deal with farmer cooperatives. The overall legal framework for farmer cooperatives, especially the Federal statutes, includes some special provisions regarding taxation, monopoly power, credit, research and other features. Many of these legal provisions have financing implications.[2]

It should be noted further that this study is concerned primarily with the financing of marketing, purchasing, and farm business service cooperatives organized under the general statutes for cooperatives referred to above. It is concerned only incidentally with cooperatives organized under special Federal laws (such as the electric and telephone cooperatives supervised by the Rural Electrification Administration) and with those credit cooperatives supervised by the Farm Credit Administration which finance individual farmers. There are some features of the special cooperatives, however, which will have significance for the financing of farmer cooperatives generally. Likewise, the book will be concerned with cooperatives serving general consumers and special non-farmer groups only when a special advantage would be gained by studying their experiences.

The present status of farmer cooperatives in the United States has evolved over a period of more than 150 years. In summarizing this growth, the Farmer Cooperative Service divided it into five broad stages of development:

> The first period, beginning shortly after 1800 and ending about 1870, was one of experimentation; the second from 1870 to about 1890 resulted

---

[1] These distinguishing features of farmer cooperatives are set forth in greater detail in *Three Principles of Agricultural Cooperation,* Farmer Cooperative Service, Educational Circular 13, November 1958.

[2] While legislative provisions affecting farmer cooperatives change from year to year, three references giving historical and basic legal foundations for agricultural cooperatives may be of interest. For a short statement see Raymond J. Mischler, "Agricultural Cooperatives Have Legal Foundations," *Farmer Cooperatives In The United States,* Farmer Cooperative Service, Bulletin 1, December 1955. The early evolution of cooperative legislation in the United States was presented effectively by Edwin G. Nourse in *The Legal Status of Agricultural Cooperation* (The MacMillan Company, 1927). A more recent and detailed statement was prepared by L. S. Hulbert and revised and extended by Raymond J. Mischler in *Legal Phases of Farmer Cooperatives,* Farmer Cooperative Service, Bulletin 10, January 1958.

from Grange stimulation; the third from 1890 to 1920 saw the rapid organization of business cooperatives; the fourth from 1920 to 1933 was characterized as orderly commodity marketing; and the fifth period from 1933 to date (1955) may be described as one of emphasizing sound business principles and adapting to modern needs. This last period is marked by growth, diversification, integration, consolidation, and modernization.[3]

Most of the trends observed in 1955, when the above was written, are still under way and seem likely to continue for some time, although there have been some shifts in emphasis and some new developments. Most of this chapter will be devoted to a brief review of those developments which seem likely to have significant financing implications for the present and for the coming decade.

Shrinking Numbers of Associations—A Continuing Trend

The peak number of farmer cooperatives was reached about 1922, when 14,628 were estimated to have been in operation. While membership, services, and volume of business have greatly increased, there has been an almost continuous decline in the number of active associations since that peak. In 1937 the Farm Credit Administration, with the assistance of the banks for cooperatives, colleges of agriculture, and some state agencies, made an extensive survey of farmer cooperative organizations. The results indicated that as of 1936 there were 10,752 farmer cooperatives engaged in marketing, purchasing and related farm business services. About 7,500 associations were engaged principally in marketing, but 73 percent of them performed additional services. Another 2,538 were primarily purchasing associations, but 27 percent also performed other services. Of the 762 associations engaged in rendering services other than marketing and purchasing, cotton gins (362) were the most numerous. The total membership reported by the 10,752 associations was 3,256,000.[4]

Estimates and reports by the Farmer Cooperative Service show that by 1950-51 the total number of farmer cooperatives had declined to 10,064, and to 8,907 in 1962-63. It is anticipated that the decline in the number of associations will continue well into the future. One estimate is that the total will be down to about 7,000 by 1973.[5]

---

[3] *Farmer Cooperatives in the United States, op. cit.,* p. 10. A more detailed description of these periods is given on pp. 10-24 of this bulletin.

[4] *A Statistical Handbook of Farmers' Cooperatives,* Farm Credit Administration, Bulletin 26, November 1938. The membership statistics include duplications to the extent that farmers were members of more than one cooperative.

[5] Glenn E. Heitz, "Banks for Cooperatives," *The Next Ten Years*: Seminar Proceedings of The Federal Farm Credit Board, Farm Credit Administration, December 3, 1963, p. 36.

It is significant that although the number of cooperative associations has declined, the total number of members in these cooperatives has continued to increase up to the time of the most recent estimates. From the 3.25 million reported during the 1936 survey, the total membership was estimated to have risen to 7,091,000 by 1950-51 and to 7,200,000 by 1962-63. It is of further interest that this increase occurred during a period when the total number of farmers was declining. The United States Department

FIGURE 1

Farmer Cooperatives Organized and Discontinued, 1901-1939

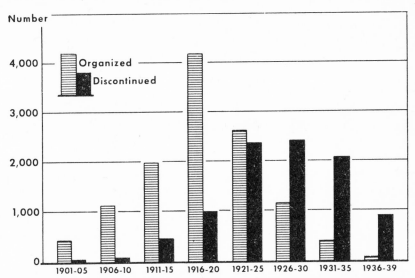

The greatest activity in both organizing and discontinuing farmer cooperatives occurred during the four decades following the turn of the century. These figures on the rise and decline in the rates of organization and discontinuance are from: W. W. Cochrane and R. H. Elsworth, *Farmers' Cooperative Discontinuances, 1875-1939*, Farm Credit Administration, Miscellaneous Report 65, June 1943.

of Agriculture has estimated that the number of farms dropped from 6.7 million in 1936 to 5.6 million in 1950, and to 3.6 million in 1963. As will be pointed out later, a factor of considerable significance to cooperatives in this trend is that the decline in the number of farms has been principally among the smaller farmers, while there has been an increase in the number of larger farms, such as those having annual gross sales of $10,000 or more.

There have been three principal reasons for the decline in the number of associations. As shown in Figure 1, thousands of associations have been discontinued. Poor management and flagging member support were major

5

factors leading to dissolution. As the weaker organizations were weeded out, business failures became a less important cause of the declining total.

Another factor contributing to the decline in numbers is that relatively few new cooperatives are being organized. While new needs and opportunities continue to appear as economic and technological circumstances change, they are usually taken care of by adding the required services and facilities to existing cooperatives. In a limited number of instances, however, new cooperatives are organized to meet the special requirements.

In recent years—and probably for quite a while into the future—the most important factor contributing to the decline in the number of cooperatives is the merger or consolidation of associations. Such combinations, together with some business discontinuances, have been exceeding the number of new cooperatives being organized, thus accounting for the decreasing total.

It should be noted that the declining numbers are not indicative of retrogression, but instead are a factor in expansion. The net effect of the elimination of weaker associations and the combining of two or more businesses into one has been a stronger structure of farmer cooperatives. The same processes have occurred in non-cooperative corporations. The fewer—but larger and better—businesses have been responsible for the remarkable growth that has characterized both farmer cooperatives and other types of corporations.

Many More Mergers and Consolidations
Are Expected

During the interviews with cooperative leaders and workers, the author found wide and emphatic agreement that there are still too many cooperatives and that their overall position would be greatly strengthened if many more mergers and consolidations were worked out. The additional strength gained from such combinations will be necessary if many cooperatives are to hold their place in competition. It was pointed out that in some situations such problems can be resolved by buying out the competitors.

Efforts to merge, consolidate, or purchase existing facilities or companies, of course, have been a dominant fact in virtually all types of business for many years. The principal purpose of such efforts has been to increase returns on capital through diversification and through vertical or horizontal expansion, by acquiring established plants or going concerns instead of undertaking the risks of construction and market development. Proven management talent also is frequently acquired in this manner. Farmer cooperatives have similar motivations, and in order to keep pace with their

6

competitors and to gain the maximum benefits for members, they too have effected many successful combinations.

The potential benefits from well-planned mergers or consolidations are well known, and numerous illustrations can be found. Two may be cited briefly, selected somewhat arbitrarily because of their convenient availability in published form. In the merger of the Farm Bureau Service Company of Iowa and the Illinois Farm Supply Company to form FS Services, Inc., in 1962, the added volume of business provided for the feed mills of the new organization had a beneficial effect on the cost of all feed purchased. Likewise, with larger volumes to deal with, the petroleum specialists were able to bargain more effectively and to achieve some product exchanges that were not available previously. In such exchanges there were savings on freight and other transportation costs. Another potential source of saving was the reduction per unit in administration costs.[6]

With similar purposes in mind, members of the Cooperative Grange League Federation Exchange, Inc., of Ithaca, New York, and the Eastern States Farmers Exchange, of Springfield, Massachusetts, voted to combine in 1964. The new organization, Agway, Inc., is headquartered in Syracuse, New York. Preliminary studies indicated a total wholesale and retail dollar volume of business in excess of $500 million, to be handled by 6,400 employees. The anticipated benefits included lower costs, better use of manpower, more research activity, savings of several million dollars, and new and expanded services.[7] Subsequently, Agway and the Pennsylvania Farm Bureau Cooperative Association voted to merge in 1965, substantially enlarging the Agway operations.

The rate at which farmer cooperatives have been combining has been increasing in recent years. Figures originating with the Farmer Cooperative Service indicate that during the five-year period 1947-52 there were 181 mergers of marketing and purchasing cooperatives, constituting 1.8 percent of the total number of associations estimated to be in operation in 1947. Ten years later, during the period 1957-62, there were 329 mergers, or 3.4 percent of the total number of associations in operation in 1957. The number of mergers and the rate of their increase during the ten years were greatest among dairy cooperatives.[8]

The data indicate further that farmer cooperatives have been very active also in acquiring non-cooperative businesses and established facilities,

---

[6] Dale E. Butz, "Measuring the Merits of Mergers," *News For Farmer Cooperatives,* Farmer Cooperative Service, February 1964, p. 14.

[7] "Members Voted to Merge Eastern States and GLF" *News for Farmer Cooperatives,* April 1964, p. 9. See also E. H. Fallon, "The Agway Story," *American Cooperation 1964,* American Institute of Cooperation, pp. 31-3.

[8] Milton L. Manuel, "The Case For Cooperative Mergers and Consolidations" *American Cooperation 1963,* p. 172.

mainly through purchase. A study by Willard F. Mueller shows that during the period 1940-55, 338 cooperatives acquired 485 other farmer cooperatives through merger and consolidation. During the same period, 337 cooperatives acquired 553 non-cooperative businesses or plants.[9] While data on the dollar amount of assets or the volume of business involved are not available, it appears, on the basis of the number of cooperatives, that acquisition of non-cooperative businesses is used as frequently as a means of growth, diversification and expansion as are mergers and consolidations.

There is little doubt that the pressures of competition and the incentives to enlarge services and increase savings for members will continue to motivate many more mergers, consolidations and acquistions by farmer cooperatives. As already stated, cooperative leaders and workers who were interviewed expressed the belief that not only are many more combinations needed but that in spite of difficulties they will be worked out. Some indication of such potentials in the dairy industry was given in a report, "Improving the Efficiency of Dairy Cooperatives in Wisconsin," made by the Governor's Dairy Marketing Committee. This report stated that in 1958 there were 262 dairy cooperatives operating 319 plants in Wisconsin, but that in the Committee's opinion 54 plants could do the job and that sales could be handled by 8 cooperatives.[10]

Services Are Being Expanded and Diversified

As just pointed out, major purposes in the mergers, consolidations and acquisitions by farmer cooperatives are to enlarge operations and to add services and benefits for members through diversification and vertical and horizontal expansion. Supplementing — and possibly exceeding — these methods of broadening services are (a) internal expansion and development and (b) joining with other cooperatives in setting up new organizations or subsidiaries to provide the added services and expansion. Investments for these purposes are a major feature of the present-day development of farmer cooperatives.

Such diversification and expansion takes a variety of forms, but is limited to those which will contribute to the production and marketing of farm products. In the case of supply cooperatives, much of the expansion has gone into the acquisition or construction of plants for manufacturing materials used by farmers, particularly into facilities for processing petroleum, fertilizer and feed products. In the petroleum field, some of the

---

[9] *The Role of Mergers in the Growth of Agricultural Cooperatives*, California Agricultural Experiment Station, Bulletin 777, February 1961, p. 22.

[10] As summarized by the chairman, Marvin A. Schaars, in "New Frontiers For Wisconsin Dairy Cooperatives," *American Cooperation 1961*, pp. 43-50.

larger cooperatives have invested in facilities which provide a vertical chain of ownership and processing, beginning with the underground oil reserves and extending to the distribution to individual farms through local affiliated cooperatives. Likewise, several of the larger supply regionals own or are acquiring mineral deposits and then mining, manufacturing, distributing, and even applying the finished fertilizer on the farm. The manufacture of mixed feeds is a major service of supply cooperatives, and certain other supplies are also being manufactured for use by farmers. As these activities expand additional warehouses, and transportation and distributing facilities are required.[11]

The supply cooperatives, furthermore, are expanding services and making required investments by adding marketing functions. Many of the larger supply regionals perform some marketing services, which are extended to farmers through affiliated local associations. As one example of such trends, the Tennessee Farmers Cooperative, a regional providing supplies distributed through local associations in Tennessee has, with the help of the Farmer Cooperative Service, studied the types of marketing functions which are needed and could efficiently be added to the activities of both the regional and the locals. The possible end result of such diversification would be to make each local association serve the complete supply and marketing needs of farmers in its territory. Such an expansion of services obviously would call for substantial investments in warehouses and other facilities.

Although some marketing cooperatives limit their services to bargaining and to negotiating sales of the products of their members, increasingly they are enlarging their services by processing and packaging, and also providing supplies used in producing the products to be marketed. Fruit and vegetable cooperatives keep adding to their already extensive facilities plants for canning, freezing, drying, packaging and otherwise processing their products and getting them ready for sale. Some associations manufacture their own cans, containers, and other materials. The dairy cooperatives, of course, have extensive facilities for preparing milk and its products for sale in both the wholesale and retail markets. In poultry marketing (both meat and eggs), the cooperatives may begin by furnishing the chicks which will become either broilers or a laying flock, providing feed for their growth, and acquiring facilities for preparing the eggs and broilers for sale

---

[11] Data on the amount of investments being made for these purposes are not readily available but some understanding of the nature of these services and the related investments by regional supply cooperatives can be gained from two publications of the Farmer Cooperative Service: J. Warren Mather, *Handbook on Major Regional Cooperatives Handling Farm Production Supplies 1958 and 1959,* General Report 89, January 1961; and J. Warren Mather and Anne L. Gessner, *Regional Cooperatives Handling Under $10 Million of Supplies 1960-61,* General Report 115, August 1963.

in retail markets. Sugar cane growers build processing plants which require substantial investments. Livestock marketing associations are experimenting somewhat cautiously in building slaughtering, freezing and even packing plants.

The construction and modernization of such facilities is a constant process. Furthermore, many of the marketing cooperatives are increasing their supply services for members. The investments required for these purposes are substantial and without doubt will be continued, probably on an increasing scale. Sometimes a separate cooperative will be organized to provide the new function and will acquire or build the needed facilities. In most instances, however, existing cooperatives initiate, construct or acquire, and finance the facilities and equipment.

Modernization and Adjustment to Change

Closely related to the investments that are being made in processing, manufacturing, storage, and distribution facilities for the purpose of adding and improving services to members are the outlays which cooperatives must make in order to keep their plants and equipment up to date and geared to the constant changes taking place in a dynamic economy. These changes affect not only the kind of equipment and plant that may be needed but also the type of service which cooperatives must offer if they are to keep pace with competition. To enable themselves to adjust more promptly to the changing technology and markets, many of the larger cooperatives maintain research departments which study both operations and markets.

The dairy industry, including the cooperatives, provides a striking illustration of constant investments necessitated by change. The shift to bulk handling of milk on the farm and in the receiving and processing plants has required extensive replacement of equipment and huge investments at both the production and processing stages. In addition to financing such changes in their own plants many cooperatives also help finance the investments which individual farmers have to make on the farms. Improvements in transportation and increases in production, as well as changes in consumer attitudes, have forced many cooperatives to construct processing plants as a means of disposing of surplus milk. Improvements in drying milk and in developing other dairy products likewise call for constant modernization of equipment.

Substantial investments have been required in other industries because of technological developments. One example is the substitution of the solvent for the crushing process in obtaining oil from soybeans and cottonseed. Cotton marketing cooperatives have installed highly efficient electronic equipment to improve classification of the cotton and accuracy in meeting definite specifications called for by buyers. Supply cooperatives

10

are building pipelines to provide a cheaper and more effective means of transporting oil from producing centers to distributing areas. Grain cooperatives are acquiring barges and building waterfront facilities in order to utilize water transportation.

Adaptations to changing agricultural production patterns are sometimes necessary. When quotas on domestic production of sugar were lifted following the Castro takeover in Cuba, several new cooperatives were organized and built processing facilities in order to have a market outlet for the increased production. The shift of cotton production from the Southeast to the Southwest had a tremendous effect on investments for handling, processing and marketing cotton and cottonseed as well as for producing it on the farms.

Other changes taking place on the farms are having an impact upon farmer cooperatives. As farms decrease in number but increase in size a cooperative serving a limited area will have fewer members but its individual transactions will be substantially larger. It is believed that in some areas this trend, combined with improved transportation, will operate to reduce the number of local cooperatives and create in their place a smaller number of relatively large distributing and marketing centers. Since such centers will have substantially greater volumes of business, they will be in a better position to utilize modern equipment, obtain a higher quality of management, and conduct operations on a more efficient basis. For example, in some of the older grain producing sections, the small and inefficient grain elevators built many years ago will be forced out of business and will gradually be replaced by fewer and larger facilities with modern grain handling equipment.

Advances in technology, the development of new products and processes, shifts in consumer preferences and many other changes are likely to continue indefinitely. In such an environment, farmer cooperatives must make appropriate adaptations if they are to hold their place in the competition. As they have in the past, these changes will call for continually increasing investments.

Development of Foreign Trade

Farmer cooperatives have made, and will continue to make, many investments in facilities and promotional efforts for the purpose of developing or expanding outlets for their products in foreign countries. Within recent years grain marketing regionals have organized two federated cooperatives to concentrate on exports. Producers' Export Company, located in New York City and owned by twenty-two regional grain cooperatives, has exported many millions of bushels of grain throughout the world. Mid-States Terminal, Inc., of Toledo, Ohio, is owned by four regionals

11

in Ohio, Indiana, and Michigan. It operates a terminal on the St. Lawrence Seaway and has handled as much as 20 percent of the grain moving through the port of Toledo. Soy-Cot Sales, Inc., owned by twenty-one separate cooperatives, was organized to sell soybeans and cottonseed products in domestic and foreign markets.

Many other cooperatives are seeking to expand foreign sales. Calcot in California, for example, stated in its 1962 annual report that it had marketing agents in twenty foreign countries. Cooperatives handling poultry, tobacco, vegetable oils, honey, dry beans and peas and other products are developing export markets for their commodities. The International Cooperative Petroleum Association, made up of cooperatives in a number of countries, including the United States, is developing international trade in petroleum products.

There is little doubt that the more aggressive marketing regionals will continue to push the development of foreign markets for their members' products. In many cases this will mean substantial investments in expensive port facilities and possibly in facilities abroad. The long range outlook is that world-wide demand for United States agricultural products will steadily increase. A detailed study by the Department of Agriculture of the long-term relationship between world population and food supplies included the conclusion that "the role of the U. S. agricultural sector, as a source of food, capital and technical assistance for the food-scarce, less developed regions is growing steadily promising to achieve an importance without precedence."[12]

Experimentation in Developing Retail Outlets

Farmer cooperatives are organized to serve the interests of agricultural producers. Inevitably, however, in building volume in furnishing supplies to farmer-members and in exploring all facets of the job of marketing farm products, there are potential business relationships with nonfarm consumers. These relationships present both opportunities and problems, and as urbanization of rural areas proceeds the opportunities and the problems become greater.

Farm supply cooperatives serving areas becoming populated by suburbanites find many new customers among these rural nonfarmer residents.

---

[12] *Man, Land and Food,* U. S. Department of Agriculture, Foreign Agricultural Economic Report 11, November 1963, p. 130. See also *The World Food Budget, 1970,* USDA, FAER 19, October 1964; and Senator George S. McGovern, *War Against Want,* (Walker and Co., 1964) in which the former director of the Food for Peace Program proposes in effect that production controls be removed and American farmers be handed the job of closing the world (mainly the noncommunist world) food gap.

Although such patronage builds business volume it raises questions as to whether the patrons should be admitted as full-fledged members of the farmer-owned cooperative, creating the possibility that voting control could pass into nonfarm hands. A further hazard in such an event is that certain tax and other advantages provided by law to farmer-controlled cooperatives might be lost.

Marketing cooperatives are interested in nonfarm people mainly as consumers of their products. In their search for dependable outlets, many farmer marketing associations have entered into contracts with large retail grocery chains and also with distributors at the wholesale level. Such contracts ordinarily call for specified qualities and amounts, and help to stabilize sales and often to increase prices because of the quality requirements and standardization. Furthermore, such contracts shorten and simplify the progress of the raw product from the producer to the consumer.

Some farmer cooperative leaders, however, believe that in developing such a relationship with the consumer market the greatest benefits to both producers and consumers can be gained in situations where producer cooperatives deal directly with consumer cooperatives, or own or control retail outlets. This arrangement applies to both the marketing of the farm products and the meeting of farm and nonfarm needs for various types of supplies.

Based upon the opinions expressed during the interview phase of this study, most cooperative leaders believe that the vertical development of producers' cooperatives should proceed, as it is now doing, through the processing steps and probably into the wholesale distributing stage, but should stop short of acquiring control of retail food stores. Two reasons usually were given, one being that the interests of producers and consumers tend to conflict. The former wish to obtain the highest possible price when selling, while the latter wish to buy at the lowest possible price. Farmer cooperatives, therefore, tend to shy away from any type of relationship which might mean that voting control would shift from the producer members to consumer members. The second objection was that control of retail outlets by farmer cooperatives would require substantial investments and would carry the risk of engaging in a business operation where margins might be relatively thin and experience in management and operations was limited.

In these circumstances, there has been only cautious experimentation by farmer cooperatives in acquiring control of retail outlets, admitting nonfarmer patrons to full membership, and developing working relationships with consumer cooperatives. One early experience of this type is the development of the P & C stores by GLF. The first store was organized in 1941, with the initial capital being furnished by the federation. It was launched "as an experiment to bring producers and consumers into the same business on a partnership basis, but the real objective was to get a start in the retail food business."[13] These stores were gradually increased in number until more than forty were in operation. They have been incorporated as a separate cooperative, with GLF furnishing a substantial part of the capital. A more recent development of this nature has been the purchase of a chain of 148 retail dairy stores by a farmers' milk-marketing cooperative in Frederick, Maryland. The possible purchase of retail grocery chains also has been studied by several large farm organizations.

A different type of experiment, designed to bridge the gap between poultry producers and consumers, is under way in California. The Hayward Poultry Cooperative (now Pacific Growers, after consolidation with Nulaid) had been marketing eggs under participating contracts with several retail food chains. The cooperative and the chains organized the Producers and Retailers Cooperative, Inc., in which the growers' cooperative and the chains each own 50 percent of the stock. This intermediary cooperative buys eggs from the growers cooperative, processes and packages them, and then sells them to the chains. Margins are determined on the basis of established market quotations, and after deducting necessary expenses and reserves the net proceeds are divided evenly between the growers' and consumers' organizations. This arrangement permits both the growers and the consumers to share in the savings.[14]

While there may be additional experimentation and investment in retail marketing, it seems likely that for some years to come farmer cooperatives, in their growth and development investments, will concentrate on the production, supply, processing, and marketing stages, stopping short of the retail level. Some farmer cooperative leaders have been concerned about the fact that grocery chains are moving into the processing and supply fields. It is their view that such functions should be developed by the producer organizations, while the retail chains and other distributors should confine their operations to serving the consumer.

Average Size and Total Business Volume Are Increasing

As a result of the types of developments and rates of growth which have been described, there have been substantial and continuing increases in the total volume of business done during recent years, and in some

---

[13] Joseph G. Knapp, *Seeds That Grew, A History of the Cooperative Grange League Federation Exchange* (Anderson House, 1960), p. 275.

[14] Elinor F. Sylvester, "Producers + Retailers = PARCO A New Type Co-op," *News For Farmer Cooperatives*, August 1963. pp. 3-17.

14

areas the cooperatives' share of the total available business has increased. Although the number of associations has been declining, the decrease has been more than offset by the increase in the average size of cooperatives.

In the last ten years for which data are available, the total net dollar value of business transacted increased 45 percent. In 1952-53, a total of 10,128 cooperatives had a net business volume of $9.5 billion of which 77 percent represented marketing services, 21 percent the sale of supplies, and nearly 2 percent other services. By 1962-63, a total of 8,907 associations had estimated gross sales of $18.3 billion and net sales of $13.8 billion, exclusive of intercooperative business. The distribution between marketing, supply, and other services was approximately the same as it had been ten years earlier.

Studies of growth made by the Farmer Cooperative Service suggest that in recent years farmer cooperatives may be more than holding their own against the competition. The data indicate that from 1954-55 through 1962-63 the value of marketings by cooperatives increased faster than the total value of farm products marketed and that, except for 1957-58, expenditures for supplies and equipment procured through cooperatives rose at a faster rate than the total expenditures by farmers for that purpose.[15]

The trend toward larger associations is one of the outstanding features of cooperative development. A somewhat superficial measure of this trend is provided by comparative figures of their average size. In 1930 average sales per association amounted to about $200,000. Not counting inter-association transactions, the sales average increased to $810,000 by 1950, and to $1,355,00 in 1962.[16]

A better understanding of the size of farmer cooperatives was provided by the Farmer Cooperative Service in a classification based on 1961-62 business volume. It will be noted from Table 1 that 2.6 percent of the total number (252 associations) had sales and services with a total value of $10 million or more, while 1.4 percent (129 associations) had a business volume of $20 million or more. The latter include six associations which appeared in the listing of the 500 largest industrial corporations in the United States in the July, 1964 issue of *Fortune* magazine.

As such sizes are attained, farmer cooperatives experience management and operating problems and capital and financing requirements similar to those of large industrial corporations. The objectives of increased size have been to expand and improve services to members, develop efficiency of

[15] Anne L. Gessner, "Cooperative Growth Trends Show Up Well," *News For Farmer Cooperatives,* March 1965, pp. 3-4 and 15-16.

[16] Anne L. Gessner, "Today's Co-ops—Fewer and Better," *News for Farmer Cooperatives,* January 1964, p. 8.

operations, acquire greater market power in buying and selling, and reap other benefits from large scale business volume. In the interviews, however, the author found no evidence of any intention to develop virtual monopoly power in the market, as was contemplated during the 1920's. The objective, rather, is to build substantial, efficient businesses which can deal on equal terms with other large traders in present-day markets. Some cooperative leaders are impatient with the current rate of development and believe that progress would be faster if there were greater cooperation among cooperatives.

TABLE 1

Size of Business of Marketing, Farm Supply, and Related Service Cooperatives, 1961-1962

(In Percent)

Business Volume (In Thousands of Dollars)	Type of Cooperative			
	Marketing	Farm Supply	Service	Total
Under 500	41.3	66.3	99.0	51.7
500 - 999	23.6	19.5	1.0	21.8
1,000 - 4,999	28.2	12.3	—	21.8
5,000 - 9,999	3.0	.6	—	2.1
10,000 - 19,999	2.0	.5	—	1.2
20,000 and over	1.9	.8	—	1.4
Total	100.0	100.0	100.0	100.0

Condensed from Table 1 in article by Anne L. Gessner, "Size of Cooperative Business Continues to Increase," *News For Farmer Cooperatives,* Farmer Cooperative Service, April 1964. The total number of cooperatives was 8,986 (marketing 5,575; farm supply 3,204; service 207).

There is a considerable interest in developing cooperatives primarily for bargaining purposes. Many of the present cooperatives, especially in the dairy field, began as bargaining organizations and then, as needs arose, branched out into processing, distributing, and other services. One of the advantages of limiting services to bargaining is that collective action can be taken with very little capital.

The evidence indicates that the trends which have been outlined so far in this chapter, will continue into the indefinite future. They should be kept in mind, therefore, when examining the financing resources and practices available for these expanding business organizations.[17]

[17] More detailed descriptions of current developments and activities of farmer cooperatives are available in the "Review" issues of *News for Farmer Cooperatives.* In recent years, the January issue has been devoted to articles, mostly by staff members of the Farmer Cooperative Service, summarizing significant developments. These reviews have been helpful in preparing this chapter.

Potential Role of Cooperatives in Agricultural Industry

There are still further developments which seem likely to increase significantly the role that farmer cooperatives will play in American agriculture. These developments include the declining percentage of the total population living on farms and the relatively rapid increase in urban population, the shrinkage in the political influence of farmers and their organizations, and the resulting difficulty in obtaining legislation for farm programs that might require substantial subsidies. Farm population had declined to 7 percent of the total in 1963 compared with about 18 percent in 1947. Moreover, the reapportionment of Congressional districts being carried out as a result of recent decisions by the Supreme Court will increase the urban representation in Congress.

The doubts raised about the long-term status of price supports and related programs were recently summarized by Dr. George B. Alcorn, director of the University of California Agricultural Extension Service, in an address to the thirtieth anniversary stockholders' meeting of the Berkeley Bank for Cooperatives:

> The majority opinion of our economists is that in the next 25 years we will see less emphasis on government price support programs, and they will become less restrictive on production. With this would come a further opportunity for more efficient farms to get bigger. It will also tend to force prices more toward the costs of the efficient farmer.
>
> Why this consensus that our long sustained programs will decrease? The major reason is the population of the United States is becoming urban and is not likely to favor government farm price support ad infinitum. They are already very near the edge of political acceptance. Further, farmers themselves under the pressure to lower costs of production are likely to forego support prices in order to produce on a scale sufficient to lower unit costs.

Given these circumstances, farmers are likely to seek even more ways to work out their own solutions than they have in the past, with less dependence upon government aid. The trend toward fewer but larger farms, with narrowing margins offset by increased volume and greater efficiency through mechanization, represents efforts in this direction. The farmers' interest in lowering costs through supply and service cooperatives and in stabilizing and increasing their incomes through marketing cooperatives is basically a form of self help designed to minimize the price-cost squeeze. As they learn through experience and from effective educational programs that such benefits may be obtained by cooperative action, farmers may look increasingly to their cooperatives and less to the Federal government in working out solutions to their problems. These circumstances,

17

together with encouraging attitudes on the part of government and other leaders, suggest that there may be opporunities for farmer cooperatives to play a greater part in the development of American agriculture and that the trends toward market power, business efficiency, and self-sufficiency will be continued.

Impacts of Growth Trends on Financing Needs

The growth and development which have been taking place and which are in prospect for farmer cooperatives may be summarized briefly as follows:

1. Farmer cooperatives, after 150 years of development, are mature business organizations with growth patterns, management capability, and size distribution comparable to those of other business groups.

2. Although the total number of cooperatives is declining, largely because of mergers and similar combinations, their total business volume and their share of agricultural business are increasing.

3. Increases in services to members and in overall growth are being achieved through the development of modern processing, packaging and distributing functions and facilities for marketing a full range of farm products and for acquiring, assembling, manufacturing, and distributing materials and supplies used by farmers.

4. International trade by cooperatives is becoming increasingly important.

5. Farmer cooperatives may play an even greater role in agricultural industry, if and as government-subsidized programs are de-emphasized.

6. There is every indication that these trends will continue indefinitely into the future.

The first conclusion that can be drawn from the foregoing review is that the cooperatives' overall requirements for capital resources are certain to continue growing, probably at an accelerated rate. While it is not possible to make reliable estimates of the requirements at any given time in the future, past trends for which figures are available may throw some light on potential future rates of increase. Previous surveys indicate that total assets of marketing and purchasing cooperatives rose from $511 million for 10,547 cooperatives in 1936 to $3.6 billion for 9,793 cooperatives in 1954, a seven-fold increase in eighteen years. Another relevant historical fact is the 45 percent increase in total business volume during the ten years ending with 1962-63, an average annual increase of 4.5 percent.

Unpublished figures suggest that the total net worth of marketing and purchasing cooperatives may have increased at an average rate of about

18

11 percent per year between 1954 and 1962, the dates of the most recent surveys by the Farmer Cooperative Service. Such a rate seems high, however, when considered in relation to other available data and estimates. At this time, it is possible to say only that the recent annual rates of increase of the total net worth and assets of all farmer marketing and purchasing associations have been, and will continue to be, somewhere between 5 and 10 percent.[18] On the basis of this projection, the total new capital (including both the owned or equity capital and the borrowed funds) needed by farmer cooperatives to sustain their growth in the years ahead, is likely to range between $250 million and $500 million annually.

In addition to forecasting continued increases in the total capital needs, the trends just reviewed indicate quite clearly a further increase in the size of individual cooperatives. This growth will mean expansion of investments in equity capital or net worth and a steady rise in the size of individual lines of credit. Such changes, of course, are comparable to the requirements of many corporations. The amount of credit used annually by some of the larger cooperatives is likely to pass the hundred million dollar level. Several cooperatives already are using, or have available, annual credit lines in excess of $60 million. It is clear that lenders financing farmer cooperatives must be prepared to meet both short- and long-term financing needs in continually increasing amounts.

Along with the growth and development that have been described have come greater management know-how, up-to-date business methods, and sound financial practices. Such cooperatives have management personnel who can deal on equal terms with those of other businesses, including lenders, in working out effective organization, operating and financing programs.

Even with the expected growth, however, most of the cooperatives in operation will be relatively small business organizations. Table 1 indicates that in 1961-62 more than half of the total number of associations had annual "sales" of less than half a million dollars. In addition to financing, many of these smaller cooperatives would benefit from informed counseling and guidance by lenders, other cooperatives, and cooperative specialists on financial management and other problems.

[18] See Joseph G. Knapp, "The Scope of Farmer Cooperatives—Present and Future," *Journal of Farm Economics*, May 1962, p. 487. Dr. Knapp, Administrator of the Farmer Cooperative Service, ventured the following estimate of cooperative growth in the succeeding 10 years: "In view of recent progress and current trends, it would seem reasonable to expect farmer cooperatives to expand at least as rapidly in the next 10 years as in the 10 years past—by about 50 percent—but this estimate may be on the low side. With public recognition and gifted leadership, a great surge forward is possible; it could double results in the physical volume of commodities handled."

Chapter TWO

Sources of Capital
For Farmer Cooperatives

As with virtually every other corporation, the farmer cooperative must have physical resources with which to operate. Manpower alone is not enough. As cooperatives provide more services and engage in more activities beyond the relatively simple function of acting as agent or broker, they must have building space, machinery, tools, trucks, automobiles, and warehouses, and money in the bank to meet expenses.

In this discussion, these non-human resources are referred to as capital. The term "capital" is used to mean the dollar value of the resources (other than people) used by cooperatives, and is therefore roughly equivalent to the total assets as they appear on the left side of the conventional statements of assets and liabilities. Thus the total capital used by a cooperative, whether owned or borrowed, will include cash in the bank, accounts receivable, other so-called "current" assets, fixed assets (land, plant, and major equipment), any investments, and all other assets.[1]

---

[1] It should be noted that the terms "capital," "capital structure," and "capitalization," are used by writers in a variety of meanings. The definition of capital given above is consistent with that of such economists as Simon Kuznets who states that "Capital is the stock of means, separable from human beings and legally disposable in economic transactions, intended for use in producing goods or income." *Capital in the American Economy—Its Formation and Financing* (Princeton University Press, 1961), p. 15. Some economists, when discussing units of wealth used to produce goods or income, treat land as a separate factor from capital. Accountants, on the other hand, often use the term "capital" to mean net worth or the excess of total

Basic Principles of Capital Accumulation

The total assets, or capital, used by farmer cooperatives have increased as services performed and volume of business transacted have expanded. All indications point to a continuation of this trend and to increasing capital requirements.

The total economy of the United States has followed similar trends. There has been a rapid growth of capital of all kinds, especially in recent decades. The rate of overall capital accumulation may be indicated by the fact that the national wealth of the United States, measured in current dollars approximately quadrupled from 1935 to 1955 and, measured in constant prices, increased by 50 percent in the ten years ending with 1955.[2] These trends have continued in the decade following 1955, and are likely to be maintained indefinitely into the future.

Since the increasing amount of assets which will be required by farmer cooperatives is closely related to—although only a relatively small part of—the tremendous requirements of the nation as a whole, it may be helpful, before examining the financing problems of farmer cooperatives in detail, to consider briefly some fundamental economic principles of capital formation and accumulation. As they have evolved in a modern industrial society, the processes and mechanics of capital formation and accumulation are very complex. These complexities, however, add up to one basic fact, possibly over-simplified here: that capital additions arise from savings.

---

assets over total liabilities. In legal discussions, the term is sometimes used to mean the par value of a stock.

There are similar variations in the use of the terms "capitalization" and "capital structure." William H. Husband and James C. Dockeray, *Modern Corporation Finance* (5th ed.; Richard D. Irwin, Inc., 1962), p. 201, state that, "The term 'capitalization' is generally used in the sense of meaning the long-term financial or capital structure." On the other hand, Floyd F. Burtchett and Clifford M. Hicks, *Corporation Finance* (Johnsen Publishing Company, 1950), p. 70, define "capitalization" as representing the number of dollars in total outstanding security issues the enterprise has created. "Capital structure" is defined as including every permanent source from which the enterprise has derived capital whether securities were issued or not. Thus capitalization would include the dollar amounts of notes payable, other long-term indebtedness outstanding, and the amount of common stock, while capital structure would include all of such long-term items represented by security instruments in the hands of investors, plus such other net worth items as reserves and surplus. The authors mentioned two other ways in which the concept of capitalization is used. "Accountants say an expenditure has been capitalized when the money spent results in the acquiring of an additional asset. In the mathematics of finance, the potential earning power of the property is capitalized to determine the present value of the property. For instance, if a certain piece of land will rent for $1,000 a year and interest rates are 5 percent, the land is now worth $20,000, the capital sum of which at 5 percent would produce $1,000 earnings."

[2] *Statistical Abstract of the United States 1964*, U. S. Bureau of the Census, pp. 346-7.

Whether for an individual, a business corporation, a farmer cooperative, a nation, or the industrialized part of the world, capital formation results from withholding part of current income from current consumption and investing or holding it in such a way that it will contribute to future production or consumption. Such withholdings or savings, when added to the previously accumulated stock of capital goods, enhance the future capacity of the individual, corporation, cooperative, or nation to turn out goods and services.

The role of savings as the basic source of capital accumulation is the fact of economic life that is most significant for this study. The details and complexities have been examined extensively, but there are only a few special points which need be mentioned here.[3] One complication is that dollar values of capital are affected by changes in price levels. It is important to know whether the data are expressed in constant or current prices. In this volume, all statistics on capital, assets, business volume, and other monetary items are expressed in terms of current prices. Another point is that accumulated capital, including current savings, may be in the form of physical goods, money or money equivalents. Any goods or money saved may be used by the savers or may be loaned or leased to others. If money is loaned, it represents a temporary transfer of the power to purchase goods or services. In this manner credit comes into the picture, and thus constitutes one of the complexities in the process of capital accumulation.

Specialized institutions to handle credit have been developed. In effect, their function is to assemble monetary savings and lend them to others who wish to make use of such savings. The processes and statistics of capital formation are further complicated by the fact that the commercial banking systems, which are the most important of these financial intermediaries, have the power to "manufacture" credit. Within regulated limits they may lend purchasing power that may not be immediately related to past savings. However, when controlled and used intelligently this "manufacturing" process adds to the rate at which capital is produced and saved.

While capital accumulation through savings is one of the major contributing factors, other requirements for economic growth must be recognized. These include continuing advances in technology, the development

---

[3] Some of the more important studies include Simon Kuznets, *Capital in the American Economy: Its Formation and Financing*, National Bureau of Economic Research (Princeton University Press, 1961); Alvin S. Tostlebe, *Capital in Agriculture: Its Formation and Financing Since 1870*, National Bureau of Economic Research, (Princeton University Press, 1957; Daniel Creamer, Sergei Dobrovolsky, and Israel Borenstein, *Capital in Manufacturing and Mining: Its Formation and Financing*, National Bureau of Economic Research (Princeton University Press, 1960); and Raymond W. Goldsmith, *A Study of Savings in the United States*, (Princeton University Press, 1956).

of skills and know-how by the people, increases in standards of living and purchasing power of consumers, and a political climate that provides incentives and an opportunity to save and invest. Still another requirement is the development of service facilities that enable the economy to function smoothly, such as effective communications, transportation, education, and—of special interest here—financial intermediaries. While they may seem elementary, these facts of modern economic life have been stressed because they are fundamental to an examination of the processes by which any group of business organizations, including farmer cooperatives, accumulate the capital which is required for growth and even for continued operation.

Major Sources of General Business Capital

When the methods of capital accumulation as they apply specifically to the business community are examined, it is found that the general principles just outlined are applicable. The main source of funds used to run a business is generally income, and the main source of capital accumulation is income diverted from immediate expenses or dividends and reinvested in permanent form in the business. This, of course, is applicable only to "going" concerns. A newly organized business must obtain its initial capital from previous savings of organizers or other investors. The established business also borrows capital to supplement that which is available from reinvested savings.

The relative importance of the various sources of funds used by corporations is indicated in Table 2 which summarizes data obtained by the Department of Commerce from corporations in the United States. It will be noted, for example, that of $63.0 billion of funds used in 1963, $37.4 billion, or nearly 60 percent, came from internal sources—that is, from retained profits and depreciation allowances. In 1960, about 63 percent came from internal sources. Other funds came from the issuance of securities or other credits representing in effect borrowings, which are the transfer of purchasing power from other savers.

The importance of retained income in corporation finance is further indicated by data given by Husband and Dockeray in their text on corporation finance.[4] These figures originated with the president of the New York Stock Exchange, who estimated that of the $240 billion required to finance corporate expansion from 1945 to 1954, two-thirds, or $160 billion, was provided by depreciation allowances and retained earnings. Of the other third ($80 billion), 75 percent was obtained by borrowings and 25 percent by equity financing (sale of stock). He estimated further that

---

[4] *Op. cit.,* p. 230.

during the succeeding decade expansion financing needs would total $375 billion, of which 60 percent would come from current income. The remaining 40 percent would be acquired in about equal parts from borrowings and from equity financing.

The foregoing figures indicate the sources of the funds used in current operations over a period of time. The relative importance of accumulated

TABLE 2

Sources of Corporate Funds, 1960 and 1963

(In Billions of Dollars)

Source	1960	1963
Total funds used	46.2	63.0
Internal sources, total	29.1	37.4
Retained profits	6.2	7.8
Depreciation	22.9	29.5
External sources, total	9.8	11.0
Stocks	3.0	.6
Bonds	5.0	5.3
Other debt	1.7	5.0
Short term, total	7.4	14.7
Bank loans	1.3	4.3
Trade payables	4.5	6.6
Federal tax income liabilities	—1.6	1.2
Other	3.2	2.5

John A. Gorman and Paul E. Shea, "Capital Formation, Savings and Credit," *Survey of Current Business,* U. S. Office of Business Economics, May 1964.

or owned capital as opposed to borrowed capital in general corporation finance may be shown further by noting balance sheet data which give sources of funds as of a given date. Such data can be seen in Table 3, which is based upon figures from Federal income tax returns of manufacturing companies having accounting periods ending in 1961-62.

The first point to be noted from Table 3 is that the major source of funds is net worth. For the entire group of 169,072 companies, the owned capital, or net worth, provided more than 60 percent of the total funds. In considering this fact, it should be noted that these are balance sheet data and therefore do not show seasonal variations. Short-term borrowings, especially, have high seasonal peaks in some industries.

A second feature of the table is that the largest companies finance their total capital needs with net worth to a greater degree than do the smaller companies. To some extent, the relatively lower net worths of the smaller companies arise from the disadvantages connected with their smaller scale

TABLE 3

Amount and Sources of Funds Used By Manufacturing Companies at End of Year 1961-62, by Asset Size Class

| Asset Class | Number of Companies | Total Funds in use[a] (In Millions) | Source of Funds (In Percent) | | |
			Net Worth	Long-term Debt[b]	Current Debt and Other Liabilities
$1-$50,000	55,559	$ 1,189	26.6	13.2	60.2
$50,000-$100,000	27,144	1,965	40.2	14.4	45.4
$100,000-$500,000	56,441	12,970	49.2	10.6	40.2
$500,000-$1,000,000	13,642	9,544	53.8	9.1	37.1
$1,000,000-$5,000,000	12,377	25,371	60.2	8.7	31.1
$5,000,000-$25,000,000	2,820	29,693	66.0	10.1	23.9
$25,000,000-$100,000,000	773	37,654	65.1	14.3	20.6
$100,000,000 and over	316	157,578	66.3	13.8	19.9

Compiled from Table 2, *Corporation Income Tax Returns* (accounting periods ended July 1961-June 1962). U. S. Internal Revenue Service. Covers all companies in manufacturing group.

[a] Total assets.

[b] Debt maturing in one year or more.

of operations. The data suggest, however, that company growth is associated, at least in part, with company policy and ability to accumulate a strong foundation of owned capital upon which to build.

Role of Net Worth in Farmer Cooperative Capital

While the general principles regarding capital sources of farmer cooperatives are the same as those which apply to non-cooperative businesses, there are also some significant differences, especially in the methods of building equity capital or net worth.[5] A preliminary view of the sources of capital for farmer cooperatives is given in Table 4. These figures, as well as those in Tables 5 and 6, are taken from a survey made by the Farmer Cooperative Service for fiscal 1954.[6] This survey, which covers data from a sample consisting of 1,157 cooperatives, provides the best information currently available regarding overall sources of capital and methods of financing. The Farmer Cooperative Service made another survey in 1962. Summary data available for the regionals included suggest that changes in general sources and methods of financing which occurred since 1954 are not of major significance.

One of the first things to be noted from Table 4 is that, as in the case of general business corporations, net worth is the most important source of capital for farmer cooperatives as a whole, providing about 58 percent of the total. Borrowed capital represented by formal documents and agreements provides 25 percent, while the other short-term obligations represent 17 percent of the total assets or capital. These are averages for all types and sizes of marketing, supply and business service cooperatives.

It will be noted further, however, that there are wide variations in these proportions, depending upon the type of cooperative—a characteristic which is also true of non-cooperative businesses. Marketing cooperatives depend more on borrowed capital than do supply cooperatives. Likewise regional cooperatives, on the average, make greater use of borrowed capital than do the smaller local cooperatives. Some reasons for these differences will be developed in the discussions of net-worth building in Chapter Four and lending policies in Chapter Five. At that time it will also be

---

[5] At this point, some additional definitions may avoid or reduce confusion. First, two classes of capital—borrowed and owned—should be noted. Owned capital is that owned by the members of the cooperative (and in some cases by others) reflecting their share of ownership in the business and usually involving no obligation on the part of a cooperative to repay the member's investment at a given date. If any borrowings by the cooperative from its members have specified maturity dates and interest rates, they are not ordinarily included with owned capital. Neither are short-term liabilities such as amounts due on products turned over to the cooperative for marketing or processing.

In this discussion, owned capital, equity capital and net worth will be used interchangeably. If the term "member capital" is used, however, it may include loans made by members to the cooperative in addition to the equity capital. In other words, "member capital" will refer to the total investment of the members in the cooperative whether the investment is loaned or owned.

One more definition belongs in this footnote. Table 4, dealing with the sources of capital for farmer cooperatives, includes "other liabilities" as one source. In effect, these liabilities can be considered as borrowed capital, since they consist mainly of short-term obligations not evidenced by formal notes or other documents (such as accounts payable, amounts due patrons for products delivered, etc.), interest accrued but not yet due, or reserves for taxes due within the year.

[6] Helim H. Hulbert, Nelda Griffin, and Kelsey B. Gardner, *Methods of Financing Farmer Cooperatives,* Farmer Cooperative Service, General Report 32, June 1957.

noted that there are significant differences in these proportions among marketing cooperatives handling different types of products.

Table 5 indicates another feature of capital sources for farmer cooperatives which is similar to those of business concerns: by far the greater share of the equity capital or net worth of cooperatives has been accumu-

TABLE 4

Equity Capital, Borrowed Capital and Other Liabilities as a Percentage of Total Assets of 9,793 Farmer Cooperatives, Fiscal Year 1954

(In Percent)

Type of Cooperative	Net Worth	Borrowed Capital	Other Liabilities	Total
Regional				
Marketing	36	45	19	100
Farm supply	64	24	12	100
Local				
Marketing	67	14	19	100
Farm Supply	79	7	14	100
All cooperatives				
Marketing	52	29	19	100
Farm supply	71	16	13	100
Total	58	25	17	100

Helim H. Hulbert, Nelda Griffin, and Kelsey B. Gardner, *Methods of Financing Farmer Cooperatives,* Farmer Cooperative Service, General Report 32, June 1957. These figures are estimates for all cooperatives based upon survey data. On March 6, 1965, the Farmer Cooperative Service issued selected data on the financial structure of 448 regional farmer cooperatives summarized from the 1962 survey. Net worth as a percent of total assets was reported as follows: 105 farm supply associations, 63.8 percent; 217 marketing associations, 53.1 percent; 34 tobacco marketing associations, 3.7 percent; 24 diversified associations, 56.4 percent; 68 bargaining and service associations, 49.1 percent.

lated by withholding a portion of the income, with a minor share obtained through the sale (usually for cash) of stock or some other evidence of a share of ownership. Referring to the average for all marketing and supply cooperatives, which includes both locals and regionals, the 1954 survey indicates that 15 percent of the equity capital was acquired by sale of securities, while 71 percent was obtained either through authorized deductions from the proceeds when members' products were sold or by retaining a part of the savings achieved for members which might otherwise be refunded in cash. In addition, 14 percent of the equity capital was obtained through some combination of purchase, deduction or retains. The proportion of the latter percentage represented by purchase is not known, but it seems safe to say that at least three-fourths of the equity capital of farmer cooperatives represented by this survey sample was accumulated through the "savings" route of deductions and retains.

The difference between authorized deductions and refunds retained should be noted. Deductions may be made by marketing cooperatives

TABLE 5

Principal Sources of Equity Capital of Farmer Cooperatives, Fiscal Year 1954

(In Percent)

Method of Acquiring Equity Capital	Marketing Cooperatives	Supply Cooperatives	All Cooperatives
Purchase	9	23	15
Withholding from sales or income			
Authorized deductions	18	—	10
Refunds retained	59	63	61
Combinations of purchase, deductions and retains	14	14	14
Total	100	100	100

Helim H. Hulbert, Nelda Griffin, and Kelsey G. Gardner, *Methods of Financing Farmer Cooperatives*, Farmer Cooperative Service, General Report 32, June 1957.

from the proceeds of products sold; for example, the cooperative may deduct and credit to a member's equity capital account an authorized amount for each hundred pounds of milk or bale of cotton marketed for him. Such deductions are not customary in the case of the farm supply operations. For them, and also for many types of marketing operations, the amounts retained come from the net income remaining after all expenses are paid and appropriate additions made to reserves.

It should be noted further that in organizing a new cooperative the initial capital necessarily must be provided by direct investment of cash by members. This form of acquiring equity capital is also used from time to time by "going" associations which may need new capital for expansion, if this method seems preferable to increasing the deductions or retains.

Sources of Capital Borrowed by Farmer Cooperatives

Although net worth generally provides the major part of their capital, farmer cooperatives would not be able to develop their services to the fullest extent without the use of borrowed funds. As already pointed out, the average cooperative finances about 25 percent of its assets by borrowing and 17 percent in the form of "other liabilities." Table 6 shows the lenders who furnished the borrowed capital reflected in Table 4. It should be noted that only 632 of the 1146 associations for which these data were obtained in the 1954 survey reported any borrowed capital as of the date of the survey. The 514 associations reporting no borrowed capital represented a variety of situations. Some operated without formal borrowings at any time because they financed all requirements with equity capital and accounts payable. They were able to do this either because of the nature of the business or because of unusually conservative policies in which services were limited to those which could be financed with owned capital. In other instances, no borrowings were reported because the data were for the end of the fiscal year when operations were at a low level and seasonal borrowings had been fully repaid. Most of these associations undoubtedly were still using some credit in the form of accounts payable, amounts due members, and items included in other liabilities.

The wide difference between local and regional cooperatives in the amount of credit used can also be observed in Table 6. As of the date of their reports, 163 regionals were using about ten times as much credit as 469 locals. The average amount per association was about $52,400 for locals and $1.5 million for regionals. This difference is to be expected, since total assets per association averaged just under $200,000 for locals and a little over $4 million for regionals.

It will be observed further from Table 6 that the banks for cooperatives were the most important source of borrowings, furnishing approximately 58 percent of all borrowed funds. In view of this major role, as well as for other reasons, special attention will be given to their services and operations as procedures and problems in financing farmer cooperatives are examined in greater detail. First, however, the nature of the other sources of credit which cooperatives use should be noted.

The second most important source of borrowings was certificates of indebtedness, ranging from a little more than 6 percent for marketing regionals to nearly 30 percent for supply regionals and averaging more than 16 percent for all associations. Such certificates bear an interest rate, have a definite maturity date, and are owed mostly to members. In some cases, they have been sold to members—and possibly to non-members—for

29

TABLE 6

Sources of Borrowed Capital of 632 Marketing and Farm Supply Cooperatives, Fiscal Year 1954

Type of Association[a]	Number of Associations	Number of Associations with Borrowed Capital	Total Borrowed Capital (In Millions)	Source of Borrowed Capital[b]							
				Commercial Banks	Banks for Cooperatives	Marketing and Supply Companies	Regional Marketing and Purchasing Cooperatives	Individuals	Insurance Companies	Certificates of Indebtedness	Miscellaneous Sources
Marketing	790	427	$151.7	11.9	66.7	.5	2.6	4.8	5.2	6.8	1.4
Locals	606	312	20.6	12.7	57.1	2.7	2.3	12.5	3.4	9.1	.3
Regionals	184	115	131.1	11.8	68.3	.2	2.7	3.6	5.5	6.4	1.6
Farm Supply	356	205	117.1	8.2	46.3	3.1	3.0	3.0	4.0	29.0	3.4
Locals	292	157	3.9	15.9	41.8	.8	4.1	18.7	3.5	10.3	4.8
Regionals	64	48	113.1	8.0	46.4	3.2	3.0	2.5	4.1	29.6	3.3
All Associations	1,146	632	268.8	10.3	57.8	1.6	2.8	4.0	4.7	16.5	2.3
Locals	898	469	24.6	13.2	54.7	2.4	2.6	13.5	3.4	9.3	1.0
Regionals	248	163	244.2	10.0	58.2	1.6	2.8	3.1	4.8	17.2	2.4

Helim H. Hulbert, Nelda Griffin, and Kelsey B. Gardner, *Methods of Financing Farmer Cooperatives*, Farmer Cooperative Service, General Report 32, June 1957.

[a] Tobacco associations excluded because of heavy borrowings from the Commodity Credit Corporation.

[b] In percent.

cash. In other instances, they have been issued as patronage refunds. Some certificates of indebtedness were reported as equity capital rather than borrowed capital, primarily because they did not carry definite due dates and were not interest-bearing; or they were carried as equity capital because they were issued as patronage refunds.

Next in importance as a source of credit were commercial banks, which furnished from 8 percent of total credit used by supply regionals to nearly 16 percent used by supply locals, and averaged a little better than 10 percent for all associations. Many local associations have established good credit relations with nearby banks. Likewise, some of the larger commercial banks have become interested in making loans to some of the larger regionals, recognizing that they would be desirable risks because of their strong financial position.

The remainder of the credit used was obtained from a variety of sources, including insurance companies (especially mutual or cooperative companies such as the Nationwide group) and individuals, many of whom are farmer-directors and members. Cooperatives also borrow from one another. Marketing and supply companies with which a cooperative deals are a minor source of occasional credit.

In a press release dated March 30, 1965, the Farmer Cooperative Service summarized the sources of borrowed funds for the 448 regional cooperatives included in the 1962 survey. This summary showed (in percent) the sources of peak seasonal borrowings during 1962 as well as the sources of borrowed funds at the end of the fiscal year 1962, as follows:

Source	1962 Year End	1962 Peak
Banks for Cooperatives	60	62
Commercial banks	11	17
Individuals[7]	20	13
Other farmer cooperatives	4	4
Other sources	3	3
Source not reported	2	1
Total	100	100

Comparison of these figures with those in Table 6, covering the 1954 survey, suggests two comments. First, commercial banks actively solicit seasonal financing for farmer cooperatives, as evidenced by their share of peak financing. Second, debenture bonds appear as a source of funds in 1962, although they were not mentioned in the 1954 survey report.

---

[7] Borrowings from individuals (in percent) were: for 1962 year end, direct borrowing 5, certificates of indebtedness 7, debenture bonds 8; for 1962 peak, 4, 5, and 5.

The 1954 and 1962 survey data did not indicate the nature of the miscellaneous sources which furnished 2 to 3 percent of the credit used. Mention may be made, however, of some sources that have furnished credit to farmer cooperatives in recent years. Around 1960, a group of cooperatives organized a mutual fund which has included loans to farmer cooperatives among its investments. A few states have enacted legislation authorizing the issuance of special bonds or in other ways assisting in the financing of industrial enterprises, including cooperatives.

Federal government credit should also be mentioned. Legislation in recent years has authorized loans to farmer cooperatives, especially cooperatives that are located in low-income areas and are unable to secure credit on a satisfactory basis from other sources. While this book is concerned primarily with marketing and supply cooperatives, the extensive financing of electric and telephone cooperatives by the Federal Government should be recognized. Governmental credit facilities available to farmer cooperatives will be discussed further in Chapter Seven.

Why the Banks for Cooperatives were Organized

In addition to their role as a major source of credit for farmer cooperatives, there are several other reasons why special attention should be given to the banks for cooperatives in this discussion. In the first place, they represent a definite stage in the historical evolution of the Federal government's interest in assisting the development of farmer cooperatives, including help in financing. A second reason is that the borrowing cooperatives are gradually acquiring ownership of the banks and within a few years will own them completely. Furthermore, as pointed out in the Foreword and the Preface, the study which provided much basic material for this book was sponsored and financed by the banks for cooperatives.

Partly for these reasons, and partly because such early history is pertinent to a discussion of the present financing arrangements, it is desirable to review briefly the circumstances and conditions which led to the decision by Congress to establish the banks for cooperatives. In the early stages of their development, financing was one of the major hurdles faced by both new and established cooperatives. Initial equity capital, of course, was obtained (as it still is) from members, either through subscriptions to capital stock or, in the case of associations which did not issue stock, through membership fees and certificates of equity. As operations got under way, deductions or retains provided additional resources. Full and satisfactory development of services, however, was not usually possible without additional capital, which would have to be borrowed. Difficulties in obtaining such credit have been described by Dr. Howard S. Whitney:

> Commercial bankers lacked confidence in newly formed cooperatives in this early period and frequently considered the corporation note as inade-

quate security for a loan. When this situation arose many cooperatives had their members give the association promissory notes, which were endorsed and discounted at a commercial bank. The notes were used as collateral to obtain both facility and working capital. The amount of each member's note was frequently proportional to the volume of business he transacted through the cooperative. Some bylaws of early cooperatives provided that to become a member, the producer must purchase a share of common stock and give the association his promissory note for a certain amount for each production unit owned.

In some cases joint notes were used rather than individual notes. The joint note was signed by several members of the association, usually the board of directors. With a joint note each individual director was actually liable for the entire face value of the note. In other cases, the bank would honor the corporation note, but would require individual notes or a joint note as additional security.

In non-stock associations the membership fees were generally insufficient to meet the capital requirements of the association. In fact, capital funds obtained through the collection of membership fees were often inadequate to provide even the physical facilities needed by the cooperative.

Early non-stock cooperatives frequently created subsidiary stock corporations to meet their facility needs. The subsidiary corporation was controlled directly by the marketing association through common stock ownership, through interlocking directorate and through a cross-contract. The subsidiary usually issued two classes of capital stock. Common stock, carrying voting privileges, was owned by the parent marketing association and non-voting stock was sold to producers and outsider investors. The capital funds realized through the sale of stock were used to purchase or construct warehousing and processing facilities. Some associations rented or leased facilities to minimize their needs for facility capital.

Working capital for operating expenses and advances to patrons was obtained through bank loans. The subsidiary issued warehouse receipts to the marketing association, which in turn pledged these as collateral with banks. The loans were retired as products were sold and the remainder of the sales proceeds was used to make final settlements to producers.

Marketing perishable products was commonly financed by the deferred payment system. This meant that producers did not receive payment until after the products were sold by their cooperative. With this system the cooperative did not need to borrow capital between the time of receiving the products and obtaining payment for them. Actually the farmers were indirectly financing the movement of the products to market.[8]

---

[8] *An Analysis of the Adequacy of Credit and Effectiveness of Credit Institutions Serving Agricultural Cooperatives, Past and Present.* A dissertation submitted to the Graduate School of the Agricultural and Mechanical College of Texas, in partial fulfillment of the requirements for the degree of Doctor of Philosophy, January 1962, pp. 57-9.

Although there were some incidental benefits to farmer cooperatives in such financial legislation as the Federal Reserve Act of 1913, the United States Warehouse Act of 1916, and the amendments to the War Finance Corporation Act of 1918 and 1921, the first real effort to improve financing arrangements for farmer cooperatives came in the Agricultural Credits Act of 1923, which established the twelve Federal intermediate credit banks. While these banks were created primarily to finance short- and intermediate-term loans to individual farmers, they were also authorized to loan to farmer cooperatives as much as 75 percent of the market value of products being stored or in the marketing stage. Between 1923 and 1956 they loaned a total of $1.1 billion of loans to cooperative associations. Their lending tapered off rapidly after the banks for cooperatives were established and ended completely in 1956 when legislation terminated this authority of the intermediate credit banks.

The next major governmental assistance in financing farmer cooperatives was included in the Agricultural Marketing Act of 1929, which provided for the establishment of the Federal Farm Board. Congress also created a revolving fund of $500 million to be used by the board in carrying out its functions of promoting the effective merchandising of agricultural commodities (in order to place agriculture on a basis of economic equality with other industries) and stabilizing the marketing of agricultural commodities and their food products. As one means to these ends, Section 7 of the act authorized the board to make loans from the revolving fund to cooperative associations for the purposes of: (a) the effective merchandising of agricultural commodities and food products, (b) the construction or acquisition of physical marketing facilities, (c) the formation of clearinghouse associations, (d) the education of producers regarding the advantages of cooperative marketing, and (e) the extension of credit to cooperative associations to permit larger advances to their members. All loans were required to be made in furtherance of the general functions of the board, and there were no restrictions on the amounts which the board could lend to individual cooperatives except in the case of loans for the construction or purchase of facilities.

During its four years of operations the board loaned $403.2 million to cooperative associations. Because of the serious depression conditions and the related fall of commodity prices, heavy losses were sustained on the loans to stabilization corporations, but losses on loans to cooperatives were relatively small. A number of cooperatives financed by the board developed into strong associations which are still operating successfully.

When a new Administration and a new Congress came into power in 1933, several important decisions were made regarding the government's role in assisting farmer cooperatives with financing. One of the first steps

34

was to consolidate into a single agency all functions relating to the super-vision of the existing Federally-sponsored agricultural credit agencies. This was accomplished by an Executive Order dated March 26, 1933, which created the Farm Credit Administration and transferred these activities to it. Its powers included supervision of the twelve Federal land banks and the twelve Federal intermediate credit banks previously supervised by the Federal Farm Loan Board (which was abolished), as well as control of the Seed Loan Agency transferred from the Department of Agriculture, the Regional Agricultural Credit Corporation from the Reconstruction Finance Corporation, and the functions and staff of the Federal Farm Board.

Another decision, one with which this book is more directly concerned, was to consolidate into a new form those activities (including financing) of the agencies transferred to the Farm Credit Administration which were designed to assist in the development of farmers' cooperatives. Accordingly, the Farm Credit Act of 1933 authorized the chartering of thirteen banks for cooperatives. Except for loans necessary to protect those previously made, no further direct loans to cooperatives were made from the revolving fund of the Federal Farm Board. Likewise, as already stated, direct loans to cooperatives by the Federal intermediate credit banks were tapered off and ended completely in 1956. The government's role in assisting with the financing of farmer cooperatives was delegated completely to the new banks for cooperatives, which were chartered during the latter half of 1933.

Functions and Operations of the Banks for Cooperatives

Under the 1933 act, thirteen banks for cooperatives were organized: twelve district banks and the Central Bank for Cooperatives. The district banks were located in the same twelve cities as the Federal land banks and the Federal intermediate credit banks. The act provided also for twelve production credit corporations, and these too were located in the same cities. The production credit corporations, however, were merged with the Federal intermediate credit banks in 1956 so that there now are three Farm Credit banks in each of these twelve cities—a Federal land bank, a Federal intermediate credit bank, and a bank for cooperatives. The Central Bank for Cooperatives is located in Washington, D. C.

Under this overall plan, the Farm Credit System is composed of three sets of financing institutions, each providing a specialized type of credit, which together furnish complete credit service to farmers and their coop-eratives. These three groups are: (a) the Federal land banks and the Federal land bank associations, which provide farmers with long-term loans secured by first mortgages on the farm real estate; (b) the Federal intermediate credit banks and the production credit associations, which furnish short- and intermediate-term credit to farmers; and (c) the banks for cooperatives, which finance farmers' marketing, purchasing and farm business service associations.

The philosophy behind this arrangement is that even though the institutions are legally separate, they are in a position to work together closely in tailoring services to farmers' needs. There are several features in the makeup of the system which are designed to encourage and implement such a relationship among the three groups of banks and local associations. In the first place, all are under the supervision of the Farm Credit Administration, an independent government agency with a single administrator, known as the governor. The governor and his staff have had a number of authorities and responsibilities conferred upon them by a series of acts of Congress, including the writing of rules and regulations relating to specified phases of the operations of the Farm Credit banks and affiliated local associations. The policies that are followed in carrying out these functions and in exercising general supervision over the banks and associations are determined by a thirteen-man Federal Farm Credit Board. Twelve members are appointed by the President of the United States on a staggered-term basis, one from each Farm Credit district. Thus far these appointees have always been chosen from among nominees selected by ballot by the stockholders of the Farm Credit banks. The thirteenth member is designated by the Secretary of Agriculture.

Another coordinating influence is the manner in which the boards of directors of the Farm Credit banks are selected. It was concluded that if the three Farm Credit banks in each city had the same board of directors, effective cooperation among the banks could be facilitated. Each district board of directors is composed of seven members selected as follows: two elected by the Federal land bank associations in the district, two elected by the production credit associations, two elected by farmer cooperatives which are stockholders of the bank for cooperatives, and a seventh is appointed by the governor of the Farm Credit Administration. Thus, with members from each lending group as well as representation of the public interest, a district board is, at least theoretically, in a position to consider the operations and responsibilities of each of the three separate banks and their related associations when meeting the total credit needs of farmers and their cooperatives.

The Central Bank for Cooperatives has a completely separate board of directors. It is composed of thirteen members, one elected from each of the twelve districts by the bank for cooperatives of that district and one appointed by the governor of the Farm Credit Administration. Another feature contributing to a democratic attitude and philosophy in the system is that each of the Farm Credit banks and associations is organized on cooperative principles.

The banks for cooperatives provide a complete credit service to eligible farmer cooperatives. Term loans may be made for the acquisition, construction, expansion, or remodeling of facilities and equipment used by cooperatives. Operating capital loans can be made to assist in financing any phase or need in the conduct of the cooperatives' general operations. The main purpose of this type of loan usually is to supplement working capital, and the loan may be made on either a seasonal or term basis. Short term loans of a seasonal nature are made also to finance the storage of practically any farm product or supply.

The main function of the Central Bank for Cooperatives is to assist the district banks in making loans which are too large to be handled within the lending limits of the individual bank. By participation with the Central Bank, and if necessary with other district banks, any district bank is in a position to handle the credit requirement of even the largest cooperative in its lending territory. The Central Bank no longer makes direct loans to cooperatives, but in addition to participating in loans it may make direct loans to district banks for cooperatives. These are usually short-term loans to meet temporary needs.

The officers of each bank for cooperatives are selected by the board of directors, but the president selects the other personnel. Each bank staff is made up of people with the variety of skills and competence required for constructive and intelligent financing of farmer cooperatives. The officers keep in close touch with cooperative developments in their respective districts. In addition to accounting and other service personnel, the staff includes credit analysts and appraisers, the latter frequently having engineering training. As the cooperatives expand services and operations into more complex and technical processing and manufacturing, the banks frequently employ consultants who are experts in the field in order that the proposed financing may be evaluated and planned more intelligently.[9]

How Banks for Cooperatives Are Financed

As in the case of any other cooperative or business corporation, the banks for cooperatives operate with both equity capital and borrowed funds. Referring first to the equity capital or net worth, it should be noted that the initial capital stock of each bank was subscribed by the

---

[9] The following publications of the Farm Credit Administration provide more detailed information regarding the Farm Credit banks and associations generally and the banks for cooperatives in particular: *The Cooperative Farm Credit System— Functions and Organization,* Circular 36A; *Loans to Farmers' Cooperatives,* Circular 6; *Banks for Cooperatives—Quarter Century of Progress,* Circular E-47.

Federal government out of funds remaining from the $500 million revolving fund which had originally been made available to the Federal Farm Board by the Agricultural Marketing Act of 1929. The first investments made at the time the banks were organized totaled $110 million. The Farm Credit Administration was given administration of the revolving fund and eventually salvaged nearly $186 million, including $24 million of interest, from the original $500 million fund. From this source additional investments were made in the capital stock of the banks, reaching a peak of $178.5 million for the years 1945 to 1954.

In 1955 legislation provided the plan now in effect, under which the cooperatives using the services of the banks, build up their investment in the banks and government-owned capital is gradually retired. Under this plan there are three classes of capital: Class A stock, which is government-owned; Class B stock, representing investments by cooperatives and others on which dividends of 2 to 4 percent are paid; and Class C stock, owned by borrowing cooperatives.

Class C stock is the most important and may be acquired in the following ways: (a) by purchasing at least one qualifying (voting) share; (b) by investing regularly in such stock a certain required percentage (from 10 to 25 percent) of the amount of interest the cooperative pays on loans from the bank; and (c) through patronage refunds paid in the form of such stock from part of the bank's annual net savings and by distribution of surplus previously allocated to borrowers on a patronage basis. In each bank, the government-owned (Class A) stock is retired annually in an amount equivalent to the Class C capital stock acquired by borrowers during the same year.

The district banks for cooperatives acquire stock ownership in the Central Bank in substantially the same manner as borrowing cooperatives acquire stock in the district banks. The Central Bank, in turn, uses proceeds from these stock subscriptions and retained earnings to retire government capital which had been invested in it.

In this manner, all of the government capital invested in the banks for cooperatives eventually will be returned to the revolving fund. At that time, except for any Class B stock which may still be held by others, the Central Bank for Cooperatives will be owned by the district banks for cooperatives and the district banks will be owned by the cooperatives that use them. This transfer of ownership to the users of the banks follows precedents set by other component parts of the cooperative Farm Credit System. After a bank for cooperatives has retired all of its government capital, the board of directors can consider beginning to revolve borrower-owned stock. However, Class C stock issued for a fiscal year period may not be retired until all Class B stock issued during or prior to that year has been called for retirement.

The method by which the banks for cooperatives obtain loan funds must also be described. The resources represented by the net worth, supplemented by short-term credits from the Federal intermediate credit banks and commercial banks, were adequate during the early years of the bank's operations. It was recognized, however, that eventually the requirements for making loans would exceed these sources of funds. Accordingly, the 1933 act provided that the method of obtaining loan funds should be that which had been used by the Federal land banks and the Federal intermediate credit banks since the beginning of their operations—namely, selling securities in the investment market.

Using this method, the Federal land banks sold bonds secured principally by the mortgage loans made to farmers, while the Federal intermediate credit banks sold collateral trust debentures secured by appropriate loan documents. These banks employed a common fiscal agent, with offices in New York City, to manage sales of their securities. On each issue or sale the interest rates, terms, and amounts were adjusted to the conditions of the market and the requirements of the banks. The bonds and debentures were not guaranteed as to either principal or interest by the Federal government, but they were classified in the market as government agency securities. As experience was gained over the years and investors became acquainted with them, their quality rating steadily improved until their status with respect to price, interest rate, and marketability was second only to that of Federal government securities.

In the case of banks for cooperatives the authority to issue debentures was at first limited to the Central Bank. From January 10, 1950, when its first issue was sold, through 1954 the Central Bank issued $300 million in debentures. On August 23, 1954, Congress authorized the issuance of consolidated debentures which would be the responsibility of all thirteen banks. This action put the debentures of the banks for cooperatives on the same basis as the consolidated bonds of the Federal land banks and the consolidated debentures of the Federal intermediate credit banks. Since that time, all debentures marketed by the banks for cooperatives have been consolidated issues. They are secured by collateral consisting of cash, government securities, and notes and other obligations of borrowers, the total being at least equal in value to the debentures outstanding. The total amount of the debentures outstanding may not exceed eight times the combined capital and surplus of the thirteen banks. The debentures are a lawful investment for all fiduciary and trust funds under the jurisdiction of the United States government and they may be accepted as security for all public deposits, including United States Treasury, tax,

39

and loan accounts. They are also legal investments for banks, trust companies, savings banks, and trust funds in the various states, and for Federal credit unions and Federal savings and loan associations.

Within a short time after the banks for cooperatives' debentures appeared on the market, they shared with Federal land bank bonds and Federal intermediate credit bank debentures the favored position of "agency" securities. The same fiscal agent handles the sale of all three groups of securities, thereby providing a total volume of business large enough to permit effective and minimum-cost marketing.[10]

In summary, Chapter Two has been concerned with the sources of capital used by farmer cooperatives. It has been noted that there are two broad classes of capital, one representing equities of members and one borrowed—either on a formal basis from lenders or as obligations on a current basis arising from day-to-day operations. Equity capital usually is obtained initially from investments by members, but by far the largest amount is accumulated through retaining a part of the income. The special problems connected with building equity capital in the form and amount needed to sustain the anticipated development and growth of cooperatives will be discussed later.

Borrowed funds to supplement the equity capital are obtained by loans from the banks for cooperatives, commercial banks, cooperative members or other individuals, other cooperatives, and miscellaneous sources. The most important source of credit, however, is the thirteen banks for cooperatives which, according to surveys, furnish more than half of the total credit used. In view of their importance as lenders, as well as for other reasons, Chapter Three will be devoted to some phases of the banks' extensive experience in financing farmer cooperatives.

---

[10] A more detailed description of the method of obtaining loan funds through the sale of bonds and debentures used by the Farm Credit banks, including the banks for cooperatives, is available in *Marketing Farm Credit Bank Securities,* Farm Credit Administration, Circular E-48.

Chapter THREE

Success Factors Revealed By the Financing of 6,300 Cooperatives

The factors determining the growth, stagnation, or failure of a farmer cooperative and those affecting the success or failure of the financing program of a cooperative are closely interrelated. While the financing program itself will influence the success of the cooperative, the same elements that govern success or failure of a cooperative also determine whether the financing program will work out satisfactorily. These basic factors of cooperative growth and effectiveness are among the first and most important considerations which a credit analyst looks at in making the evaluations that precede decisions on applications for loans.

It is appropriate, therefore, early in this study of the financing of cooperatives, to see what lessons regarding these interrelated factors have been learned from past lending experience. The greatest accumulation of such experience is in the thirteen banks for cooperatives, which for many years have been the most important source of credit for farmer cooperatives. In examining their wealth of experience, this book shall be primarily concerned with the more general factors influencing cooperative growth and effective financing.

Broad Lending Experience Available for Study

From 1933, when the banks for cooperatives were organized, to the end of 1964, they had financed about 6,300 individual cooperatives, located in 48 states and in Puerto Rico. These cooperatives were of all sizes—from the smallest locals to the largest regionals—and represented a wide variety of financial structures and conditions, types of organization, services performed, and products handled. The financing of marketing has involved every major crop and virtually all of the minor ones, as well as all types of livestock, poultry, and related products grown on farms in the United States. The banks have financed extensive supply services performed by cooperatives, especially the procurement, manufacture, and distribution of petroleum products, fertilizers, and mixed feeds. The marketing and supply operations financed have included procurement, transportation, storage, grading, processing or manufacturing, and packaging. They have also included the acquisition, expansion, remodeling, or construction of the necessary facilities, equipment, and offices. In short, there is practically no form of activity or service of farmer cooperatives that has not been financed at some time by the banks for cooperatives.

Each loan file contains a great deal of information on the cooperative, especially if the file covers several years of financing. When one of the banks for cooperatives receives a loan application, a thorough study is made of the association, not only with respect to its status as a cooperative but especially from the standpoint of its effectiveness as a business operation. The nature and extent of this analysis, of course, depends upon whether the cooperative is making its first application for a loan or whether it has borrowed before. A representative of the bank usually visits the cooperative, and if physical facilities are to be financed and will constitute part of the security, an appraisal is made.

After the loan is made, the bank follows the association's financial progress and related trends closely. A bank officer or field man calls on the cooperative from time to time. Following each such visit, or after the cooperative's representatives have visited the bank, a memorandum is written summarizing the discussion, giving information developed, and reporting any significant plans or developments. Annual and other reports of the cooperative are added to the file. At the end of the year (if a new loan program is set up), or whenever an additional loan is requested, there is a review of past operations, a comparison of actual performance with previously made plans and budgets, and consideration of the plans and projections for both the immediate and long-range future. The file also includes a record of loan committee decisions and the deliberations and reasons behind them.

Thus the loan files have become a vast storehouse of information regarding the operations of individual cooperatives and the factors that affect their degree of success. Officers, credit analysts, attorneys, appraisers, and field representatives of the banks likewise accumulate a great deal of personal knowledge about farmer cooperatives. During their service with the banks, they have opportunities to observe the operating problems of numerous associations, to learn why they succeed or fail, and to recognize elements of weakness or strength.

In view of the necessity of maintaining the traditional confidential relationship between borrower and lender, the lessons and information derived from this experience have necessarily been restricted to use by directors, officers, and other personnel of the banks for cooperatives and by the immediate supervisory staff in the Farm Credit Administration. One purpose of the study made for the banks for cooperatives was to attempt to distil from all of this experience the most significant lessons and principles regarding the general operations and financing of farmer cooperatives, so that they could be made available to those interested without violating the confidential nature of the material.

Carefully Selected Loan Sample Studied in Detail

Access to this immense amount of information presented an unusual research opportunity but àt the same time necessitated the formulation of a plan of study that was manageable within the time and resources available. It was clear that it would be a physical impossibility, and also unnecessary, to examine all of the 6,300 loan files in the banks' records. Accordingly, it was agreed that a detailed study of a carefully-selected sample of loans would be sufficient.

It was decided that the sample should be drawn from the files of cooperatives which had been financed by the banks for cooperatives during relatively recent years, for the most part since 1950. The principal reason for this limitation was that problems and decisions that will be facing cooperatives and lenders in the years ahead are more likely to be similar to those encountered in recent experience than to those of twenty or thirty years ago. While the information developed in the sample cases included early historical material when it was pertinent and the cooperative had been in operation for a considerable length of time, the detailed analysis and information concentrated on recent experience. In each loan history in the sample, a study period was selected for this more intensive examination, usually covering the latest available ten years of operations.

For this part of the overall study of the financing activities of the banks for cooperatives, a sample of 350 accounts was selected. The general characteristics of this sample may be observed in Table 7. In working out the method of selection, it was decided that the sample should include representation from the most common and significant situations which have been and will be involved in applications for loans received by the banks. As indicated by Table 7, six such situations were defined, as follows:

1. Growth. Cooperatives that had a rate of growth and development well above average.

2. Deterioration. Cooperatives that had gone downhill, sometimes ending in liquidation but in all cases involving some losses to members.

3. Recovery. Cooperatives that for some reason had become weakened seriously but later were restored to financial health.

4. Low-equity financing. Cooperatives having a relatively small amount of net worth in relation to borrowed capital.

5. Newly organized. Cooperatives organized by farmers or by other farmer cooperatives in recent years.

6. Mergers, etc. Cases where cooperatives merged or consolidated, or where cooperatives acquired facilities or a business from non-cooperative organizations.

It will be noted from Table 7 that each of the six subdivisions of the sample includes both regional and local cooperatives, and that there is a reasonably good distribution among types of services. There is also wide geographic distribution, since selection by the twelve district banks was made for each subdivision from both regionals and locals and from different types of services. No case studies were furnished by the Central Bank, because it does not make direct loans to individual cooperatives. The sample, furthermore, has good size distribution, ranging from small locals to the largest regionals. The cases were selected by the banks in accordance with instructions stating the requirements just described. Their selections were reviewed critically by the Cooperative Bank Service to determine whether, judging from the knowledge of its staff members concerning cooperative activity throughout the United States, the sample was adequately representative.

After the sample was determined, a detailed loan history and analysis was prepared by each bank on every account drawn from its files. These case studies followed a uniform outline which had been approved by the Planning and Advisory Committee supervising the study. The outline included pertinent early history, balance sheets, income and expense statements, and similar data covering operations during the study period. The nature of the operations and the problems which were met and over-

TABLE 7

Number of Farmer Cooperatives in the Financing Study Sample, by Subdivision and Major Type of Service

Nature of Sample	Total Cooperatives	Supply Cooperatives	Marketing Cooperatives						
			Grain	Cotton and Cotton-seed[a]	Fruit and Vegetables	Dairy	Poultry	Livestock	Miscellaneous[b]
Growth									
Regionals	24	8	6	5	1	2	1	—	1
Locals	47	7	9	4	9	12	2	—	4
Deterioration									
Regionals	7	5	—	1	—	1	2	—	—
Locals	55	7	15	4	16	6	2	—	5
Recovery									
Regionals	7	3	—	—	—	2	—	1	1
Locals	38	5	16	4	4	7	—	—	2
Low Equity									
Regionals	17	3	4	4	—	3	1	2	—
Locals	43	4	13	3	8	7	2	—	6
Newly Organized									
Regionals	11	3	1	4	—	2	—	—	1
Locals	48	12	9	7	4	3	3	2	8
Mergers, etc.									
Regionals	9	3	2	—	—	4	—	—	—
Locals	44	5	10	3	6	19	1	—	—
Total									
Regionals	75	25	13	14	1	14	2	3	3
Locals	275	40	72	25	47	54	10	2	25
Entire Sample	350	65	85	39	48	68	12	5	28

In this classification it is recognized that many cooperatives perform other services in addition to that under which they are classified in the table.

[a] Includes cotton ginning.

[b] Includes associations with services involving frozen food lockers, fur farming, credit, sugar, coffee, tobacco, beans, nuts, hay, mushrooms, and forest products.

45

come were discussed. Probably most important of all was the analysis section, in which the bank was requested to evaluate the cooperative generally and with the benefit of a "hindsight" view, rank in order of importance and discuss in reasonable detail the major factors which contributed to the growth, deterioration, recovery, or other characteristics of the association.

These case histories were an extremely valuable source of information about cooperative operations and financing. All case material, of course, has been kept on a strictly confidential basis, and no identifiable information from the loan files which relates to individual cooperatives has been or will be published. Additional information was obtained from the banks through conferences with officers and reports on specialized subjects.

Preliminary Generalizations

Anyone who is familiar with the history, development, and problems of farmer cooperatives will find little that is new or original in the principles derived from the analysis of these case studies. Most of the findings have long been recognized by experienced farmer cooperative leaders and workers. One of the major problems of cooperative development over the years has been making these principles known to farmers and members who become directors or find themselves in positions of leadership. This storehouse of experience confirms the validity and importance of the truisms which have long been the basis for such cooperative education.

A few preliminary generalizations, supported by study of these 350 loan histories, may be mentioned first. One which has been repeated so often that it has become a cliché, is that the management, operation and financing of a farmer cooperative must be on a business basis, and that the basic principles governing its success or failure are fundamentally the same as those determining the fortunes of any other kind of business. There are, of course, some differences in the laws and restrictions under which cooperatives must conduct business, and such differences must be recognized. But within these limits, cooperatives must raise necessary capital, develop an adequate volume of business, and control expenses so that there will be some margin or savings, just as any other business operated as a profit-making concern must do.

Recognition that a farmer cooperative must be run on a business basis is one of the first requisites in obtaining capital from investors and lenders. An enthusiastic belief in, and expectation of, benefits from the cooperative way of doing business are helpful but are not enough. Theory and practice of cooperative philosophy must be accompanied by sound business methods. This is an elementary but primary requirement to successful financing.

A second point to note is that there are no sacred formulas or ratios which govern loan decisions or which assure financing and operating success for every cooperative. This sample shows that there are some basic principles which must be recognized and followed. The significant fact, however, is that each cooperative is a separate entity with its own individual objectives, resources, and problems. The operating decisions and financial planning, therefore, must take account of the special circumstances of the individual case, and both operations and financing must be tailored to meet these circumstances.

The foregoing point leads to the related generalization—again reflecting study of the 350 loan histories—that decision-making in lending to farmer cooperatives is simply a process of evaluating the special circumstances that affect the success or failure of the applicant cooperative and its capacity to repay the loan desired. The first step in reaching a decision consists of assembling as completely as possible the information pertaining to the cooperative: its management, membership, financial status, nature of operations, and record of past performance if it is an established association. This step also includes the proposed operating and financing plan, with appropriate projections and budgets. The second step is to evaluate this information, including particularly the basic factors that may determine the cooperative's success or failure. Following these evaluations, there is a decision by the members of the loan committee reflecting their seasoned judgments. Some factors may be weak, others strong. Decision-making thus is a process of forming sound conclusions as to net outlook in view of the particular combination of strong and weak factors.

Characteristics of Growth Cooperatives

In attempting to summarize what may be learned from past financing experience, the histories of the cooperatives in the growth group will be examined first. These associations were selected because they progressed and expanded faster than the main body of cooperatives. Using changes in dollar amounts of total assets as a measure, the average (median) annual rates of growth during the study periods were 29 percent for regionals and 26 percent for locals. Such rates, of course, are substantially in excess of the average, not only for all cooperatives but for general business corporations as a whole.

As noted in Table 7 the growth sample consisted of twenty-four regionals and forty-seven locals, a total of seventy-one associations. The regionals included some of the largest farmer cooperatives in the United States, and there were some fairly large locals. There were also some small associations with assets of only $300,000 to $400,000. Most of these cooperatives had been in business for a considerable period, but some were relatively new. At the time of the study the regionals varied in age from six to forty-two years. The oldest locals were organized in 1908 and 1909 while the newest began operations in 1951 or later.

A preliminary observation suggested by study of the growth sample is that when the basic factors are right, farmer cooperatives have a capacity for growth that is nearly equal to that of comparable non-cooperative businesses. But they have at least one limitation that must be recognized: in expanding or diversifying their services to members, cooperatives are generally confined to furnishing supplies or services needed in producing agricultural products or in processing and marketing them, or with furnishing business services to farmers. Non-cooperative corporations, including competing agribusinesses, need not necessarily limit their products or services to the line or even the industry in which they began operations. They may expand either vertically or horizontally into almost any other service, product, or industry which appears to have potential for increasing the rate of earnings. Many non-cooperative corporations owe a substantial part of their growth and size to diversification into lines which fit in well with the organization but involve products or services having little if any relationship to the original or primary function of the business. Studies of recent business combinations and acquisitions indicate that diversification is one of the most important motives for acquisition of one business by another.

To a degree, this difference sets some boundaries on the growth potential of farmer cooperatives. The growth sample shows, however, that in spite of this limitation farmer cooperatives have demonstrated a capacity for growth virtually equal to that of other business corporations. In achieving that growth, the cooperatives in this sample used practically every method of expanding operations and services available to business enterprises generally. Not all of the associations used all of the methods, although some of the largest used nearly all of them.

Beginning with the initial function of the cooperative, growth was in either of two directions, or in both. Existing services were improved and enlarged. Improvements have included better quality or grading, better packaging, reduction of costs or more effective merchandising and sales efforts, depending on the nature of the business. The expansion was related to the improvements and resulted from increases in business done per member and in number of members. Nonmember business might also be developed.

A second method of growth has been to add services or to diversify. Frequently, such additional functions were byproducts or other services that rounded out the original activity. For example, a dairy cooperative was initially organized to improve quality and disseminate market information with respect to the animal food milk powder produced by the member associations. Then it expanded into marketing products for its members, including particularly butter. Various other services and improvements were added later.

A frequent type of diversification has been for marketing associations to add the furnishing of supplies, especially supplies connected with the product or products marketed, and for supply associations to begin marketing functions for their members. A regional originally storing and marketing cereal grains, for example, added soybeans and flaxseed to the products handled; then it diversified further into marketing livestock, manufacturing and distributing feed and other supplies, and furnishing auditing, bookkeeping, insurance, credit, legal, research, and public relations services.

Growth, whatever its direction—expanding existing services or diversifying into additional services—requires increased plant capacity and other physical equipment. These cooperatives used nearly every possible method of enlarging their physical facilities, including: leasing a plant or equipment; building additions to existing structures; replacing old machinery with larger capacity, high-speed modernized equipment; constructing a new plant; buying established businesses; merging or consolidating with other cooperatives; and organizing or joining with other cooperatives in creating subsidiaries to provide facilities for specialized purposes.[1]

Management, the Most Important Success Factor

In the growth sample of seventy-one cases the banks invariably ranked competent and aggressive management as by far the most important single factor responsible for the outstanding success of a cooperative. Almost without exception, this was the conclusion by the bank in its analysis of a case. Among the adjectives used in describing such management were "alert," "astute," "outstanding," "excellent," "capable," and "aggressive."

Top ranking of management as a success factor, of course, is neither a new idea nor an unexpected conclusion. It has long been recognized as being of major importance in the successful administration of any kind of organization, including farmer and other types of cooperatives. The analyses reconfirmed this well-established conviction.

---

[1] An excellent and detailed story of how GLF (Cooperative Grange League Federation Exchange) attained its commanding size and influence through the use of virtually all of these methods is told by Joseph G. Knapp in *Seeds That Grew,* A History of the Cooperative Grange League Federation Exchange (Anderson House, 1960). This was published prior to the consolidation of GLF and Eastern States into Agway, Inc.

The term "management" as freely used is a broad and somewhat vague word which undoubtedly means different things to different people. For example, in his opening remarks as chairman of a panel discussion on "Modern Management, Including Directors and their Responsibilities" during the 1962 session of the American Institute of Cooperation, Kenneth N. Probasco said that "management has been defined briefly as getting things done through people." He also quoted a definition by Lawrence Appley, president of the American Management Association, to the effect that "management is personnel administration."[2] As used by the analysts preparing these case studies, however, the term "management" seemed to cover a wider range of qualities and activities than are suggested by these definitions. Its full significance therefore needs to be examined.

In the first place, the reference in most cases was to the general manager of the cooperative, and this was especially true for the smaller associations. In many instances, it appeared from the analysis that the manager was the real leader and provided the main spark in the progress of the association. In other cases, especially in the larger cooperatives (and comparable to the situation in most large non-cooperative business corporations), the reference was to management as a team made up of the executive officers and including frequently the board of directors. A considerable number of the case studies stated that the general manager and the officers had the advantage of being supported by a strong board.

There were many phases of the operations of these cooperatives which, according to the analysis by the banks for cooperatives, reflected superior capabilities on the part of the management. First of all, in accord with the definitions given above, it included good judgment in selecting and supervising people. Although the various elements of successful management were carried out by many people, the spark and direction came from the top. Other factors in good management included effective direction of general operations to obtain low cost but high quality products or services; ability to recognize or anticipate change, and sound judgment in making adjustments in techniques, products, and services; well-organized promotional plans; good public and member relationships; alertness in spotting opportunities for beneficial mergers or other combinations; effective programs for employee and director training; and, last to be mentioned but of major importance in this discussion, a sound program of financing and financial management.

In the sense used in these loan analyses, therefore, management is a very comprehensive concept and, as shall be seen later, usually has con-

[2] *American Cooperation 1962*, American Institute of Cooperation, p. 25. Mr. Probasco is executive vice president and general manager of the Landmark Farm Bureau Cooperative Association, Inc., Columbus, Ohio.

siderable influence on the other success factors. Because of its prominent role, it becomes one of the most important considerations by the credit analyst when preparing information and recommendations for the loan committee.

Other Essentials for Growth

While capable management was clearly the most important requirement for successful growth, there were many other contributing factors, which appeared in a wide variety of forms and combinations. Generally, however, they can be grouped under three heads: economic need, membership support, and adequate financing. Although these factors will be discussed in that order, it does not necessarily mean a corresponding ranking in importance, since it would be difficult if not impossible to support any specific ranking.

Economic need has long been recognized as a prerequisite to the successful operation and growth of a cooperative. No business concern can succeed unless there is an effective market for its products or services. This fact of business life was strongly reaffirmed in the reports. The point cannot be stated quite as simply as that, however. The loan histories also brought out forcefully that economic need is not a static situation. On the contrary, in a dynamic society there are constant changes in markets, technology, and production methods and patterns. In these circumstances, capable management again becomes extremely important, because of the need for recognizing and even forecasting such changes and intelligently adapting the operations and services of the cooperative to them. In the growth group management was successful in making such adjustments.

The growth cooperatives also were characterized by having good membership support. Growth is dependent upon members for two vital types of support. In the first place, they must provide a volume of business of sufficient size to permit economies in handling, buying or selling, and other phases of operations. Sometimes business volume is increased through nonmember patronage, but the main dependence must be upon the patronage of members. In many of the cases studied, members contracted in writing to provide a specified volume of business to the cooperative.

Members are also the main source of equity capital. There are two forms of such investment. First, if it becomes necessary to sell stock or some other form of evidence of ownership (either when the cooperative is organized or later to help finance expansion), members will be the principal and perhaps the only buyers. They must be willing to support the cooperative by such purchases. Second, as net worth is increased by deductions from sales proceeds or retained net income, members must be willing to let such equities remain in the cooperative as long as the need for capital continues.

The loyalty of the membership is closely related to the character of the management. Members are more likely to support their cooperative if they have confidence in its management. Such confidence can best be established and maintained when members can see tangible evidence of successful operations. Another important means of building and maintaining confidence is a well-planned educational program including a continuous flow of information regarding the operations and performance of the cooperative. Both of these are the responsibility of the management and are carried out through the specialized staffs developed for those purposes.

Adequate financing is the last—but not necessarily the least—important element of success. Such financing involves both the building of an appropriate foundation of net worth and the establishment of confidence by lenders so that borrowed funds will be available on reasonable terms.

Since such financing is to be the principal subject of the remainder of this book, it will be sufficient to say at this point that the cooperatives in the growth sample were able to build the foundation equity capital at rates or in amounts required to support the growth. With such basic net worth and with good overall financial planning and management, they were able to obtain whatever credit was needed to round out capital requirements for growth. In fact many, if not most, of the loan case studies indicated that the cooperative could have borrowed more if it were necessary.

It may appear an over-simplification to have reduced the success requirements to four factors: capable management, economic need, membership support, and adequate financing. It is true that a variety of other circumstances and conditions contributed to these success stories. In some instances there was even some good luck involved. By and large, however, these four stood out as the basic elements. This will become even more apparent as the experiences of other, less-fortunate cooperatives in the sample are examined.

Why Some Cooperatives Go Downhill

As noted in Table 7, the sample included sixty-two cooperatives (seven regionals and fifty-five locals) that lost ground during the periods covered by the loan histories. These study periods, as previously stated, were in most cases about eight to ten years in length, with an extreme range of three to nineteen years. It will be significant to compare the experience, characteristics, and contributing factors in these cases with the success stories just discussed.

More than one-half of the associations in this group had deteriorated by the end of the study periods to the stage where they had ceased operating. Eleven had been foreclosed, nineteen went into voluntary liquidation or bankruptcy, and two were merged with other cooperatives. In thirteen instances the bank for cooperatives sustained a loss, the largest on a single loan being a little over $600,000. The remaining thirty cooperatives were still operating at the end of the study periods but the loans represented problem accounts for the banks for cooperatives concerned. The banks, of course, were actively counseling with the managements of these associations, and it appeared from the analyses in the case studies that possibly half of them had reasonably good prospects for eventual recovery.

It is significant to note the age of the associations in this deterioration group. Except for two local grain marketing associations for which the year of organization was not reported, the following shows the period or decade when these cooperatives were organized:

Year of Organization	Number of Cooperatives		
	Total	Locals	Regionals
Before 1920	5	4	1
1920-29	11	9	2
1930-39	14	13	1
1940-49	21	18	3
1950 and after	9	9	0
Total	60	53	7

Only nine of the sixty were organized during the more competitive recent years. About one-half of both the regionals and the locals had been in operation for twenty years or more before deterioration began. The case histories indicate that most of these associations operated successfully or satisfactorily for a period of years and sometimes for an extended length of time before trouble developed.

A further characteristic of this group is that the associations were relatively small in size, especially when compared with those in the growth group. That is to be expected, since the cooperatives selected to illustrate growth would naturally have grown larger than those which had deteriorated.

Study of these loan histories shows that a wide variety of factors and circumstances contributed to the downward trends. While no two situations were exactly alike, each having its own combination of causes, the varied contributing factors nevertheless may be grouped into a few general sources of trouble.

One of the most important difficulties was the failure or inability of an association to adapt to changes in the economic and technological environment. As has been previously emphasized, such changes have been sweeping in virtually all types of businesses since World War II, particularly in agriculture. In some cases, cooperatives were confronted with a shift in the type of farming done by its members, with the result that the economic need which the association was originally set up to serve disappeared or substantially changed. Some cooperatives organized to serve cotton producers failed to reshape their services when cotton production moved westward and was replaced by grain, livestock, or other types of production. The changes in production, processing, and marketing patterns for fruits and vegetables, milk and its products, poultry, eggs, and other products have presented adaptation problems for the cooperatives serving such growers, and some of the associations in this sample did not keep abreast of the changes. Their managements either were not sufficiently alert to the necessity for adjustment, or they were unable to cope with the problems presented.

Another major—and possibly more important—general cause of deterioration represented in this group may be described as ill-advised or disastrous management decisions. Such unfortunate actions sometimes were based on inaccurate or incomplete information, or on an erroneous appraisal of markets and outlook. In some cases, too little research preceded a major investment, or the research was not done by competent people. Some new cooperatives were organized under such conditions, and some existing cooperatives organized new facilities or departments to fill a presumed economic need that did not develop to the degree necessary for profitable operation. In other instances, management made major changes in operation—including large investments in plant and facilities—which turned out to be costly errors in business judgment. Usually in cases of this kind the association found itself saddled with excess, high-cost plant capacity and unable to shift to alternative uses or find other solutions. The accompanying operating losses eroded working capital and net worth, thus compounding the problems facing the management.

To a degree, the two general causes of deterioration which have been discussed represented management shortcomings. Management made unfortunate decisions and then was unable to cope with the consequences, or it failed to adapt successfully to the changes in production, marketing, or technological conditions. The largest group of cooperatives in the sixty-two case histories, however—possibly half of the sample—could be classified as cases in which the management simply failed, without having had to

54

face special problems or circumstances such as those already described. These inadequacies had a variety of forms and combinations. There were at least three instances in which weak management was combined with dishonesty or with falsified records or accounting. Another type of situation was that in which good accounting and record-keeping had not been developed so that management was hampered by unreliable and incomplete operating and financial statistics.

For several associations in this group, a critical weakness lay in the credit policies. Under conditions of sharp competition, management may be tempted to relax credit policy in order to stimulate sales. In such competitive circumstances, furthermore, margins are likely to become narrower. The freezing of working capital into accounts receivable and the reduction of net margins were a combination responsible for the weakening of several cooperatives furnishing supplies to their members. A related situation was that in which unusual inventory accumulations tied up working capital. The conditions leading to inventory accumulation were often related to those which built up receivables.

The most frequently observed evidence of incapable management in this sample was that of inefficient operations in general. Such weaknesses were reflected in high cost operations, inept business judgments and decisions, slowness in recognizing and eliminating unprofitable services or branches, declining volume of business, and fading confidence and support on the part of the membership.

Another factor playing a part in the decline of some associations in this group was the character of the board of directors and even of the membership itself. The analyses indicated that in more than a few cases the weak management was the direct result of a weak board of directors. Frequently, the board was ineffective because a substantial number of its members had little experience in business matters or had no real interest in or loyalty to the cooperative, even to the point of not supporting it with their patronage. Under such circumstances, the directors were unable to fulfill their responsibilities in setting objectives and goals, approving budgets, measuring performance and maintaining controls over operations. Supplementing the experiences described in these case studies, it may be added that the importance of a competent board is recognized by most cooperative leaders and has stimulated extensive educational and training programs for directors by cooperative, governmental, and educational organizations.

It is especially significant to note the role of financial management in this deterioration sample. It will be recalled that one of the characteristics of the associations in the growth group was a strong net worth position and a good program for building and maintaining adequate foundation equity capital. In the deterioration sample, most associations had a relatively strong net worth structure at one time but ended up in a weak position following several years of loss operations and general deterioration. This change in net worth position during the study periods is indicated by the following classification of the associations in the deterioration group according to the percentage relationship between net worth and total assets:

Net Worth as Percent of Total Assets	Number of Cooperatives[3]	
	Beginning of Study Period	End of Study Period
70 or more	17	4
60-69	8	8
50-59	12	7
40-49	13	7
30-39	5	7
1-29	5	20
Deficit net worth	0	7
Total	60	60

Several comments regarding the role of financing in contributing to the deterioration of these cases seem warranted. In the first place, inadequate net worth was definitely a factor contributing to the deterioration in a number of instances. Insufficient "free" funds (funds not committed with respect to maturity dates or interest charges) is a serious handicap to any business concern. It limits particularly the cash flow, making it difficult to meet payrolls, pay for supplies, and meet other current obligations. In several of the case studies, the bank for cooperatives recognized that the association was under-capitalized when the first loan commitment was made, but the bank felt justified in undertaking the financing because of the urgent economic need and because of the outlook for favorable operation and the plans for building equity capital seemed satisfactory at that time. However, management's performance and other factors did not measure up to expectations. Consequently, the combination of a weak financial position and lack of strength in other areas led to the downward trend.

A related point is that if there should be an unfavorable change in the other major factors of success—in the quality of management or the market situation, for example—a strong net worth position is not necessarily enough by itself to save the situation. Such a position will give the association financial reserves so that it will have some time in which to correct the difficulties or work out a solution. But unless the troubles are

---

[3] Excludes two cooperatives, for which figures would be meaningless because of falsified or non-comparable data.

resolved in the time so provided, insolvency may not be prevented. In any case, the former strong position is likely to be eroded, and financial problems will be added to the other difficulties.

A final comment regarding the deterioration group is that in probably a majority of the cases the causes of deterioration and the failure to remedy unfavorable situations are traceable ultimately to the board of directors and the offices of the management. Management and the board, of course, cannot be responsible for "act of God" type of disasters nor for the impacts of general shifts in technology or in economic conditions and markets. But there are differences in the ways in which weak and strong managements meet such situations and, of still greater importance, there are differences in the soundness of judgment with which day-to-day decisions are made and in the general effectiveness with which operations are conducted. The study of this sample confirms the observation made about the growth group: that capable management and a competent board of directors are by far the most important success factor.

Rebuilding Weakened Cooperatives

The lending experience of the banks for cooperatives includes many instances in which a farmer cooperative in a weak financial position was restored to economic health. As shown by Table 7, the loan case sample included seven regionals and thirty-eight local associations illustrating such situations. Although six of these associations were relatively new, having been organized in 1950 or later, most of them had been in operation long enough at the time the case histories were prepared so that their experience included first a period of building strength, then the development of trouble, and finally a recovery stage.

The reasons why these cooperatives, became weakened are very similar to those which caused the associations in the group just discussed to lose ground. In the analysis portions of the loan histories prepared by the banks for cooperatives, incompetent management was mentioned as the most important single factor responsible for the downhill trends. Such statements were made in more than half of the cases. Further factors contributing to deterioration were changes in economic and other conditions, unfavorable investment or operating decisions, natural disasters, inadequate equity capital, and generally inefficient operations. These factors appeared in various combinations, sometimes in addition to weak management and sometimes as independent causes.

In analyzing the factors which were primarily responsible for the reversal of the downward trend in the affairs of these cooperatives, several influences stand out clearly although the order in which they will be mentioned does not necessarily represent the ranking of their overall importance. A lender is likely to take an increasing interest in a borrower when it appears that the account may be developing into a problem loan. Consequently, it was noted that the banks for cooperatives were very active in attempting to diagnose the nature of the difficulty and in counseling with the management regarding remedial measures. The loan histories indicated considerable variation in the amount of guidance by counseling and suggestion or by lender-dictated requirements on the part of the banks. This variation depended in part on the willingness of the board of directors and the management to cooperate with the banks and on the ability of the manager and the board to plan and carry out their own solutions.

The specific steps taken to bring about recovery were, naturally, related to the reasons why the cooperative got into difficulty. Since weak management was diagnosed as the most frequent major cause of decline, the most common initial step taken to remedy the situation was to make changes that would improve management capability. In many of these instances, the bank for cooperatives assisted the board of directors in locating a new manager. In most cases, the board of directors at least consulted with the bank before making its final selection of the new man.

Depending upon the reasons for deterioration, other remedial steps included eliminating unprofitable enterprises, improving market outlets and marketing arrangements, altering the policy in making advances on crop receipts at harvest time, tightening up operations and reducing costs, working out mergers or reorganizations, building membership support, and increasing volume.

Regardless of the nature of the remedial steps, adequate working capital was a requirement. Since, during the deterioration stage, net worth and working capital usually had been reduced to critical levels, the recovery program necessarily included plans for restoring the financial position. The counseling and cooperation of the principal creditor, the bank for cooperatives, were especially important in this part of the recovery program. In some instances, stand-by arrangements were worked out with other creditors. The net-worth rebuilding phase, of course, was adapted to the circumstances of the individual situation, but it included the establishment or increase of some form of deductions or retains, the sale to members of additional stock or certificates of indebtedness, and continued financing support by the bank for cooperatives. Sometimes the latter method involved rearrangement of the maturity dates of outstanding indebtedness in order to give the association time to work out its problems. In other instances, additional credit was necessary.

A concluding observation regarding the problems faced by cooperatives under circumstances such as those in this sample, is that the importance of the role of the principal creditor should be re-emphasized. Obviously, in order to protect its investment, such a lender will take an active hand in counseling with, and even dictating requirements to the board and the

management. For the best interests of both the cooperative and its creditors, such a lender must be informed about the economic and technical
aspects of the operations of the borrower and must also be familiar with
and sympathetic to the cooperative form of doing business. This informed
assistance protects the investment of the lender and conserves the equities
of the members of the cooperative, as well as contributing to the recovery
of the association so that it can provide needed services on a continuing
and efficient basis.

What About Low-Equity Financing?

The financing experiences which have been discussed so far in this
chapter have indicated the importance of adequate net worth or equity
capital. One rough rule-of-thumb which many lenders use as a guide is
that the creditors should not have a greater investment in the business
than the owners. Another way of expressing this is to say that net worth
should be equivalent to about 50 percent of the total amount of assets.

While the advantages of strong net-worth positions are recognized and
emphasized, the lending experience of the banks for cooperatives includes
many instances in which cooperatives having relatively low net-worth ratios
have been financed. The sample shown in Table 7 includes seventeen
regionals and forty-three local associations which were financed on what
may be termed a low-equity basis. The outcome in these instances throws
some light on net worth policies that should be followed by farmer cooperatives and that should be required by lenders who may finance such
cooperatives.

The sixty cooperatives in the low-equity group were well distributed
as to age and size. There were variations with respect to the stage in the
cooperative's history at which the low-equity financing took place. Some
had low equities at the beginning of the study periods, while others had
relatively high equity-capital ratios at the beginning but deteriorated to
a low-equity basis during the period covered by the loan history. The
variations in the outcome of these classifications of low-equity financing
cases may be summarized briefly as follows:

Nature of Experience	Number of Cooperatives		
	Regionals	Locals	Total
Low net-worth ratio at beginning			
Made progress	10	15	25
No improvement	2	5	7
Too new to determine trend	2	9	11
Favorable ratio at beginning			
Expansion reduced ratio	2	11	13
Low earnings reduced ratio	1	3	4
Total	17	43	60

Before commenting on this experience, it would be appropriate to ask: Precisely how low is low equity? How much net worth in relation to total assets did the cooperatives in this sample have? In answering these questions, it should be stated that the classification into the low-equity group was made by the banks for cooperatives, and it was the judgment of the bank officers that these cooperatives at some stage in their histories did not have sufficient net worth to support the normal requirements of those specific types of operations. Hence there is no precise percentage of total assets (as for example, the 50 percent mentioned above) which is the dividing point between "low-equity" and "adequate-equity" capitalization. In the case of the forty-three associations that were classified as having a low net-worth ratio at the beginning of the study periods, about half a dozen had net worth above the 50 percent level on the date the balance sheet was available. Most, however, were below the 40 percent level, and about a dozen were at or below the 25 percent level. One association had a deficit net worth during the entire study period.

It will be noted that of the forty-three associations with low initial net worth, twenty-five made progress and strengthened their financial positions during this study period and seven showed no improvement, while eleven of the associations had been organized so recently that there was not enough experience to indicate a trend. There were seventeen associations in the sixty-case sample which had a favorable net-worth ratio at the beginning of the study period but later, for two reasons, changed to a low-equity position. In thirteen of these instances, aggressive managements pushed expansion at a rate exceeding that at which net worth was increased. Acquisition of facilities involved in such expansion was financed more by credit than by net worth. Consequently, the net-worth ratio declined to less than conventional levels. In the other four cases, unsatisfactory operations reduced earnings to the point at which net worth declined or did not keep pace with the growth of assets.

The experiences and risks involved in financing farmer cooperatives which have less than the conventional amounts of net worth are worthy of considerable attention and might be discussed in great detail. The most significant conclusions, however, may be summarized in four general points.

1. The experience demonstrates that conventional ratios of owned to borrowed capital, while desirable, are not an inflexible prerequisite to successful growth and financing. It demonstrates that there are circumstances in which credit can be granted with constructive results to farmer cooperatives having relatively low amounts of net worth. When credit is granted in such cases, the information regarding the cooperative must

be accurate, and the judgments regarding the adequacy of the other factors which may contribute to the success of the cooperative must be sound. In the case of the twenty-five cooperatives that made progress in spite of low net-worth ratios at the beginning of the study period, all of these other factors were "right" or very favorable. In the case of the seven which showed no improvement, there was some weakness in addition to the inadequate net worth.

2. The other factors that must be strong in order to assure success in spite of any handicap from a weak net-worth position are the same ones that stood out as significant factors of success in the other groups of cases previously discussed. A highly-capable management directing an efficient operation that turns out products or services for which there is an effective demand, plus a membership that furnishes a good volume of business and is willing to go along with a program for strengthening the net-worth position of the cooperative, is a combination likely to represent a good lending risk even though it may have less than the conventional amount of equity capital. This fact is demonstrated by the cases under discussion and by other accounts in which similar circumstances prevail.

3. In view of the foregoing generalizations, a third conclusion should be that there is no specific level, ratio, or percentage relating to net worth which can be established as the minimum requirement before making a loan commitment. The conventional 50 percent level is a desirable guideline. In actual lending practice, however, and in the financial management policies followed by many cooperatives and other business organizations, there are deviations from this "standard." Some cooperatives use no borrowed funds except those represented by current liabilities. In the discussion regarding the growth group, it was indicated that some of the large cooperatives (especially some of the regionals) have a policy of financing most of their term- or fixed-capital requirements with net worth. On the other hand, as seen from this sample and as will be noted again in the discussion of financing newly-organized cooperatives, worthy associations are frequently furnished credit in such a way that the borrowed funds exceed those representing net worth. As has been said several times, each cooperative is a separate situation, and decisions must be made on the basis of evaluations of the particular circumstances in the individual case.

4. At the same time, this experience and the foregoing comments should not be interpreted as minimizing the importance of an adequate net worth. Such adequacy is essential, not only as a basis for credit but also as a foundation for successful operations and growth. Even when other factors are favorable, the lack of strong foundation capital is a

61

distinct handicap to a cooperative. The basic difficulty of such a situation is that if the amount of "free" capital (capital having no fixed interest cost) is relatively small, the amount of borrowed funds must be correspondingly larger if the total amount of capital required for the job is to be made available. Large amounts or proportions of borrowed capital add greatly to the risk that the income will not be large enough and stable enough to cover both operating expenses and the interest and principal payments on the borrowed funds. Such interest and principal payments will be "fixed" as to time and amount and therefore must be paid when due. Any uncertainty over the adequacy and dependability of income to cover these fixed charges adds to the risk to the lender. The greater the degree to which required capital is in the form of net worth that is free of fixed interest or dividend payments and principal maturities, the more comfortable will be the operating position of the cooperative. The association will also be in a better position to compete with agribusinesses which may have capital with a relatively low fixed cost.

Financing New Cooperatives

Although there has been a downward trend in the number of farmer cooperatives, largely because of numerous combinations of associations and a few liquidations, some new cooperatives are being organized every year. A great many of these are financed by the banks for cooperatives. The 350-case sample in Table 7 included eleven regionals and forty-eight local associations which had been organized in recent years. The significant points regarding the organization and financing of these new cooperatives should be noted in this review of the experience of the banks for cooperatives.

Since many cooperative leaders feel that there are too many cooperatives, especially in certain industries, and that more mergers and consolidations are needed, it is important to determine the circumstances under which still more cooperatives are being organized. A first point is that the associations in this sample illustrate the well-established principle that a cooperative should be organized in response to an economic need. These needs, for the most part, are the product of a dynamic society. They arise from changes in economic or technological conditions or consumer preferences. Changes in competitive conditions or in methods of doing business may also be contributing factors. In these circumstances, some existing business concerns—including cooperatives—may become outmoded, while at the same time a demand for new or different services is created. When changed conditions become apparent and the possibility of savings for farmers seems well-established, the new needs may be met either by expanding or diversifying the services of existing cooperatives or by organizing new associations to serve specific purposes. This sample is comprised of instances where the decisions were of the latter type.

Expanding, and to some extent altered, needs of farmers for commercial fertilizers was the occasion for organizing some new cooperatives to produce specific types of fertilizer material. A typical procedure was for several supply cooperatives to subscribe to the capital stock required to furnish the initial net worth resources. Other associations were organized because of changes in the type of farming in their areas. In one case, cotton production had been replaced by rice production to such an extent that it became feasible to organize a separate association to serve the rice growers. In areas where fur farming has developed, it has been found that the assembling, mixing, and storing of the best kind of feed for fur-bearing animals, as well as the marketing of the pelts, can be accomplished effectively by cooperative organization. Such cooperatives are represented in the sample. In other instances dissatisfaction with existing local services led farmers in the community to organize a cooperative and take matters into their own hands. In some of these cases the new cooperatives purchased existing facilities, while in other instances they constructed the required plant. The sample includes cotton ginning and grain marketing associations organized under such circumstances. Several associations represent efforts to consolidate the business of a number of individual farmers and individual cooperatives, in order to improve marketing services and, particularly, to increase bargaining power in the markets. In some instances, a new cooperative became engaged in processing as a means of improving marketing service.

Following the decision to organize a new cooperative, the method of raising the basic risk capital and other capital needs must be worked out. Since the sample consists entirely of associations financed by the banks for cooperatives, it is not surprising to find from a study of the loan histories that representatives of the banks participated in these early discussions. They conferred about organizational details and were particularly active in planning both the owned and borrowed capital financing programs. Since one of the most difficult parts of the financing program usually is the raising of the initial equity capital, it is extremely important to obtain the counsel of experienced lenders at this stage, not only because of their knowledge in the general field of financial planning but also to enlist their interest in supplying the capital which must be borrowed.

There are several significant points to be noted from the following summary, which shows the amount of net worth or equity capital which had been accumulated by these new cooperatives at the time of the first loan by the bank for cooperatives:

Net Worth as Percent of Total Assets	Number of Cooperatives		
	Locals	Regionals	Total
Under 10	3	1	4
10-19	3	1	4
20-29	7	4	11
30-39	8	1	9
40-49	5	2	7
50 and over	22	2	24
Total	48	11	59

There may be some surprise at the extent of the low-equity financing, especially for new organizations with no previous experience. In cases in which the operations were of such a nature that they did not require a large amount of net worth, other financing did not necessarily represent high-risk lending. In one of the lowest equity cases, the members of the new cooperative were financially strong organizations which agreed to subscribe additional capital if and when required. In most of the lowest equity cases, the new association was affiliated with, and backed by one or more well-established, responsible cooperatives. In one case, a dairy cooperative organized primarily as a bargaining association found it necessary to enter into processing, which required financing of the facilities. Because of a miscarriage of the initial arrangement for financing the plant construction, the bank for cooperatives increased its commitment beyond the normal net-worth relationship in order to help save the organization. In this instance, as in many others, the undercapitalization was offset by good management, strong member support, and the cooperation of the affiliated regional.

As illustrated by these cases, each of the new cooperatives presented a special problem which required individual evaluation of the surrounding circumstances before a decision could be reached regarding the loan. The fact that so many cooperatives in this sample were started on a low-equity basis adds emphasis to the general problem of accumulating initial equity capital. It also demonstrates, as did the low-equity sample discussed above, that the banks for cooperatives do not adhere inflexibly to the 50 percent net-worth ratio which is the conventional guideline, but instead consider each case on its merits and exercise their best judgment after evaluating all the factors concerned.

Since these were newly-organized cooperatives, only a short term of experience—usually two or three years of operation—was available to indicate whether or not they would be successful. Within that period, one of the fifty-nine cooperatives in the sample had been completely liquidated because of losses, two others had become problem loans, and for about six others the future looked cloudy. There was not a high correlation however, between this record and the amount of initial equity capital. The association that was liquidated began with less than 20 percent of its assets represented by net worth, but after several years of operations it had accumulated sufficient additional net worth to reach a ratio of about 50 percent, while the debt owed the bank for cooperatives amounted to 28 percent of total assets. The reason for liquidation given in the analysis, was not inadequate financing but "crop failures resulting from freezes, together with the lack of member loyalty." The other associations which developed trouble during the period covered by the loan histories were not all in the lowest equity classifications. Those with limited initial net worth were handicapped because of a shortage of working capital, but the basic difficulty usually stemmed from other deficiencies, such as the ones seen in the other groups of loan cases.

Special Features in Mergers and Acquisitions

As was pointed out in Chapter 1, farmer cooperatives have been active in working out cooperative mergers and consolidations, and acquisitions of non-cooperative businesses in order to gain the benefits which result from such combinations. It was also indicated that in recent years the combinations of cooperatives have been taking place at an increasing rate. The banks for cooperatives have financed many such mergers, consolidations and acquisitions, and it was therefore appropriate that the sample of loan case histories included nine regionals and forty-four local associations to illustrate such financing experience.

Study of this sample shows that the decision-making process on the part of the lender, as well as the general servicing and loan experience involving cooperatives which acquire assets and functions in this manner, differ little from cases in which expansion and diversification are achieved through internal growth and development. In both instances, previous performance records must be evaluated. Various aspects of the new combination of facilities and operations must be projected carefully. The ability of the management to handle the larger scale of operations must be considered and the best judgment exercised with respect to the advisability of furnishing credit in the light of the available information, projections, and estimates.

In more than two-thirds of the cases, the principal purpose of the merger, consolidation, or acquisition was to increase the volume of business. The benefits expected from the larger scale of operations included increased efficiency and lower unit costs, obtaining (or having the capacity to obtain) more competent management, better service to members, and more power in the market to negotiate purchases and sales. Other incentives included elimination of duplicated services and of competition between the organizations being combined; recognition that the competitive situation or other local circumstances allowed little possibility of building business volume to a size which would make it competitive; and increased efficiency resulting from diversification or from combining complementary operations. There were a few cases in which a weak cooperative was saved by combining it with a stronger organization.

When a cooperative acquires non-cooperative facilities, financing differs little from that used when one non-cooperative business purchases another. The variety of financing devices used may be illustrated by a case (partly hypothetical) in which a cooperative purchased all of the capital stock of two small businesses in order to expand the total volume of its business and to provide diversification. The total investment required for this transaction was approximately $2,660,000, which was financed as follows:

Bank for cooperatives loan to pay debt of purchased business	$1,200,000
Cash from owned working capital	300,000
Unsecured note to vendors, payable at $100,000 per year	700,000
Open account credit	460,000
Total	$2,660,000

In other words, as this case shows, the purchase of a non-cooperative business by a cooperative may be accomplished by a purchase contract with the vendors who thus provide the credit, by financing with cash resources already available, or by borrowing from a conventional lender, or by a combination of two or more of these methods.

Referring next to mergers or consolidations, a special feature is that the equities of all the members in the cooperatives being combined must be fairly evaluated and then redistributed so that the new equities will have a value consistent with the value of the share which each member had in the original cooperatives. This valuation and redistribution process is greatly simplified if the use of book values is acceptable to everyone concerned. If book values are not dependable or acceptable, however, appraisal of assets and accurate information on liabilities will be required. The analysis of these cases shows that here again each situation is a special problem and that no generalized procedures can be derived which would be applicable in all cases.[4]

Two other points illustrated by this sample of loan histories are worthy of mention. One is the well known difficulty in getting managements, boards of directors, and even members to agree on what is to be done. Discord may arise over the decision to merge or consolidate or, after such decision has been reached, over the basis or terms of settlement.

The other feature which should be noted is the role that may be played by a major financing agency such as the banks for cooperatives. In these cases, the banks frequently took the initiative in bringing the cooperatives together, helping to reconcile differences and in effect serving as the catalyst that finally achieved a needed and happy solution.

Success Factors Summarized

The most important lessons revealed by this analysis of lending experience by the banks for cooperatives may be summarized as follows:

1. The effectiveness of a financing program is closely related to the factors influencing the growth and effectiveness of the cooperative financed.

2. The loan histories show that capable and alert management, including the board of directors, is clearly the most important factor in the success of a cooperative.

3. Other important factors are: keeping abreast of changing economic needs; good membership support; and adequate financing.

4. Adequate financing begins with a good program for building and maintaining foundation capital—that is, equity capital or net worth. There is no rigid formula for determining the amount of such capital, but it should be adequate to meet the specific needs of the individual cooperative.

5. The banks' experience shows that when the above factors are favorable, a cooperative has no difficulty in obtaining needed credit.

Well-informed cooperative leaders and workers will probably not find much that is new in these conclusions. Furthermore, there was so much similarity among the main lessons indicated by the six categories of cases

---

[4] The following published articles may be of interest in connection with this step in working out mergers or consolidations of farmer cooperatives: David Volkin, "Financial Problems and Procedures in Mergers," *Mergers for Stronger Cooperatives*, Farmer Cooperative Service, Reprint 208, April 1961; Alton J. Morehouse, "Accounting Aspects of Cooperative Mergers," *Cooperative Accountant*, Summer 1963; and W. R. Boniface, "Financial Aspects of Cooperative Mergers," *Cooperative Account-ant*, Summer 1963.

that the points may have seemed repetitious and belabored. There is, however, significance and advantage to the reiteration of these lessons. In analyzing the experiences of cooperatives in several different situations the result was that no matter what the conditions, virtually the same conclusions could be drawn concerning the reasons why cooperatives succeed or fail. Such consistency firmly establishes the validity of the principles and confirms the previously recognized requirements for successful cooperative operation and growth. These results also throw additional light on some of the major considerations and problems in financing farmer cooperatives.

It is necessary now to examine these considerations in greater detail. This examination will continue to draw heavily upon the experience of the banks for cooperatives, but will also use other sources, including the views of cooperative leaders expressed during the survey which was part of the original study made for the banks for cooperatives. This more detailed examination begins in Chapter Four which deals with problems encountered by farmer cooperatives in building and maintaining an adequate structure of net worth, or equity capital.

Chapter FOUR

Equity Capital Problems

Adequate equity capital or net worth is one of the basic requirements in an effective financing program for farmer cooperatives, just as it is for other types of business corporations. In fact, the accumulation and maintenance of the proper amount of net worth is probably the most important—and perhaps also the most difficult—part of the financing program for most farmer cooperatives. Generally, adequate net worth is not only the major source of total capital, but is also a standard requirement made by lenders. Still another reason for giving special attention to equity capital problems is that the difficulties of farmer cooperatives in building and maintaining the net-worth foundation needed for growth seem to be increasing.

In these circumstances, many questions are being asked about this phase of financing farmer cooperatives. Why is equity capital so important or necessary? How does a cooperative determine the amount which it should have? What are the best ways to build needed net worth? Do farmer cooperatives have greater difficulty in building net worth than non-cooperative corporations? Why can't borrowed funds be substituted more extensively for equity capital?

It is difficult, and in some cases impossible, to give positive answers to all of these questions, one reason being that the answers must be tailored to the circumstances and needs of the individual cooperative. There are also differences of opinion on certain aspects of the problems. Consequently, each cooperative must work out the solution which seems best for its situation.

Role of Net Worth in Financial Management

In considering these problems, a proper first step is to define the terms. The total capital or total assets of a farmer cooperative or other corporation may be divided into two main classes, owned capital and borrowed capital. The definitions begin, then, with the statement that net worth is the owned portion. Expanding this somewhat, it may be said that net worth is the risk capital provided by the proprietors of a business. In the language of the accountant and the financial analyst, this may be expressed as follows:

> Net worth may be considered a technical liability from a bookkeeping standpoint. It is a liability to a legal entity such as to a proprietor, to partners, or to stockholders who own the stock of the corporation. The net worth is the amount of funds invested at the risk of a business enterprise. More formally, it is a liability of a business enterprise to those interested in it after all debts of every description have been paid. The *net worth* is a single item with that exact caption in a proprietorship or partnership. Sometimes, however, it is also termed *proprietorship capital* or *partners' capital*. In a corporation, it consists of the sum of any or all of the following items that may be found in a particular balance sheet:
>
> 1. Preferred or preference stock
> 2. Common stock
> 3. Class A, B or C stock
> 4. Capital surplus
> 5. Retained earnings (surplus)
> 6. Undivided profits[1]

It is important to note from these definitions that net worth not only represents the investment of the owners of the business but also provides the primary risk capital. This fact is brought out again in a definition having specific application to farmer cooperatives:

> In a broad sense the equity capital of a farmer cooperative may be defined as its net worth. Thus, equity capital is the investment, exclusive of loan capital, members have in their cooperative. Such investments may or may not bear interest, and may or may not have a definite maturity date. Included in equity capital are such balance sheet categories as common

---

[1] Roy A. Foulke, *Practical Financial Statement Analysis* (5th ed.; McGraw Hill Book Company, Inc. 1961) p. 113.

stock, preferred stock, memberships, certificates of equity, book credits, and reserves.[2]

This definition is illustrated more specifically by Table 8, which summarizes the components of equity capital as reported by the cooperatives · included in the 1954 survey.

A qualification should be noted in connection with that part of the definitions reading "Such investments . . . may or may not have a definite maturity date," and in connection with the item in Table 8 "Certificates

TABLE 8

Kinds of Equity Capital Reported by 1,157 Marketing and Farm Supply Cooperatives, Fiscal Year 1954

(In Percent)

Kinds of Equity Capital	Locals and Regionals	Local Associations	Regional Associations
Common stock	19.2	19.1	19.2
Preferred stock	21.9	14.3	23.6
Certificates of equity with maturity dates	8.3	2.5	9.5
Allocated capital credits without maturity dates	39.1	48.2	37.1
Unallocated reserves	10.1	13.8	9.3
Membership certificates	.2	.7	.1
Miscellaneous equity and current net margins	1.2	1.4	1.2
Total equity capital	100.0	100.0	100.0

Helim H. Hulbert, Nelda Griffin, and Kelsey B. Gardner, *Methods of Financing Farmer Cooperatives,* Farmer Cooperative Service, General Report 32, June 1957, p. 9.

of equity with maturity dates." The managements of some cooperatives believe that even though such member-owned investments carry an obligation to pay at a definite time, they may properly be regarded as equity capital. Among accountants, however, there is a widespread view that any certificate of interest having a stated maturity date is an obligation in the nature of a loan, and that even though it is owed to members it should not be classified as net worth. Furthermore, a lender, when considering

---

[2] Helim H. Hulbert, Nelda Griffin and Kelsey B. Gardner, *Methods of Financing Farmer Cooperatives,* Farmer Cooperative Service, General Report 32, June 1957, p. 8.

the risks of financing a cooperative, will give less weight to the net-worth section of the balance sheet if it includes investments having specified maturity dates. This is particularly true if there is a reasonable possibility that such dates may conflict with maturity dates on the loan.

With these definitions in mind, it is possible to examine the reasons why proprietor or risk capital is needed in a business. Why not run it entirely, or almost entirely, on borrowed capital?

In the first place it must be recognized that there have occasionally been businesses, including farmer cooperatives, which began operations and even had successful growth on little or no initial investment by the proprietors or members. When this is done, virtually all of the risks of loss are borne by the lenders and other creditors. There have been a few exceptional instances in which farmer cooperatives financed in this manner have had successful operating and growth experience.

On the other hand, there are some cooperatives which, because of the nature of the business or because of the conservative policy followed by the board of directors, carry on their operations with scarcely any use of borrowed funds. This situation is frequently referred to as "overcapitalization." In such instances, obviously whatever capital is required to run the business comes from equity investments by members or other net-worth sources. Such cooperatives, since they must have enough net worth to meet practically all their capital needs, represent the opposite extreme from those which operate largely on borrowed funds.

The normal pattern, however, is to supplement the resources represented by net worth with borrowed funds. This suggests the first major reason why there must be a certain amount of net worth: namely, it is usually a principal prerequisite to obtaining credit from conventional lenders. Such lenders, making normal-risk loans at market rates of interest, cannot afford to lend under circumstances where there is likelihood or even reasonable possibility of not receiving the full interest charged or not having the full amount of principal of the loan repaid. Conventional lenders, therefore, require that their loans be cushioned by enough risk capital (net worth) to safeguard them against loss resulting from unforeseen circumstances and from errors in the original judgment of the basic credit factors. This may appear to be an elementary statement, but it is a fundamental fact of life in business finance.

Most businesses, including farmer cooperatives, have good years and bad ones, with accompanying fluctuations in net income. During bad years, a business may have trouble making interest and principal payments on loans unless it is cushioned with adequate amounts of "free" capital that calls for no fixed interest, dividend, or other payments. Such net-worth cushions protect lenders against loss in at least two ways. By decreasing the amount of fixed charges on borrowed funds which must be paid from net income, they provide greater capacity to meet direct expenses and still have enough income left to meet debt service requirements. Furthermore, if the bad years result in actual operating losses, an adequate amount of net worth should provide a cushion which will absorb the losses and leave enough so that the business can qualify as a credit risk and continue regular operations.

In addition to absorbing shocks from bad years and disasters, a substantial net worth gives management more flexibility in managing finances, even during normal times. The more total capital that comes from net worth, the lower will be the fixed charges on borrowed funds and, as a result, the greater will be the net income available for use in day-to-day business. This arrangement gives management greater freedom in carrying out plans, provides a larger flow of liquid funds for quick action if opportunities arise, helps to maintain a comfortable working-capital position, and usually makes the cooperative less dependent on banks or other lenders for long-term funds.

A strong net-worth position, however, puts the association in a more favorable position to negotiate with lenders if credit is needed. It is particularly advantageous when the cooperative is planning an expansion program. If a substantial part of the capital in normal use is furnished by net worth, there are likely to be fixed assets or other investments which are relatively free and available as collateral for term financing. The plant or equipment acquired with the new credit will add to the net income, of which a part will be earmarked for retiring the loan. After a substantial reduction in the debt has been achieved, the net worth will have increased correspondingly and equity in fixed assets will be available to support the next expansion stage.

A final consideration, and an important one, is the interrelationship between membership support and member investment. Willingness to invest in their cooperative is one evidence of good membership support. Moreover, if members have a substantial monetary stake in the business which they own, they are more likely to take an active interest in its progress and to support it with their patronage.

Net Worth Needs Are Part of Financial Plan

The foregoing reasons for having substantial proprietorship capital in a business seem fairly obvious, and most businessmen recognize the necessity of foundation equity capital. The more difficult questions have to do with the amount of such capital that a farmer cooperative should have and how it can be best obtained. There is no simple answer to either of these questions. The solutions to such problems depend upon circumstances, the nature of the operations, the stability and economic outlook of the industry involved, and other considerations.

The first step, therefore, in developing answers to these questions is the formulation of a financial plan for the particular business, and this is equally applicable to farmer cooperatives and to other types of businesses. Regarding the role of financial planning, including its relation to equity capital problems, a recent treatise on corporation finance had this to say:

> Financial planning is the key to successful business operation . . . The source of capital, because of its strategic position, exercises tremendous influence upon the success of an enterprise; but it is only a part of the larger criterion of sound business operations. In the last analysis, this is determined by the self-supporting or self-sustaining character of any particular enterprise. The real question is whether its output is sufficient to replace or retire the investment as well as to cover the attendant current demands incident to operation. The latter consists of the usual operating expenses plus a fair return to those providing the capital. The financial plan must recognize and facilitate these ultimate and more controlling demands of business. Flexibility must be maintained at all times, and the need for financial readjustments must be faced realistically.

> The most effective means of providing flexibility is found in recognizing the importance of the ownership equities. Despite the absenteeism that exists because of the number and scattered location of stockholders, the ownership account constitutes the anchor of a financial plan. In the same way in which the equity of an individual in his home gives resilience to protect the security of the mortgage, the ownership, or equity, in a corporation provides leeway to meet the "ups and downs" of business activity. The equity in a corporation consists of the stock, reserves, and surplus; and these may be adjusted in varying degrees to meet adversities.[3]

As the above quotation implies, the financial plan for any business, including farmer cooperatives, necessarily involves conversion of all aspects of the operation into dollars and cents. As L. A. Crawford, president of the Berkeley Bank for Cooperatives pointed out when discussing the subject at a meeting of the American Institute of Cooperation,[4] financial planning includes the present and projected cost or value of the assets required, budgets of expected income and expenses, cash flow projections, sources of capital funds (assets) required, and projected balance sheets. In mak-

---

[3] William H. Husband and James C. Dockeray, *Modern Corporation Finance* (5th ed.; Richard D. Irwin, Inc., 1962), pp. 201-205.

[4] Later printed as "Managing Your Finances," *American Cooperation 1961*, American Institute of Cooperation, pp. 59-63. See also Paul Bishop, "Capital Budgeting and Evaluation," *The Cooperative Accountant*, Summer 1963.

ing such projections and plans, consideration must be given to pertinent economic, technological, and other external factors. One of the end products of this process, of course, will be an indication of the total resources required to carry out the proposed plan and, further, what proportion of these resources should be obtained by building net worth and what by borrowing.

FIGURE 2

Ten-Year Projection of Capital Requirements
Southern States Cooperative, Inc. 1959 Plan

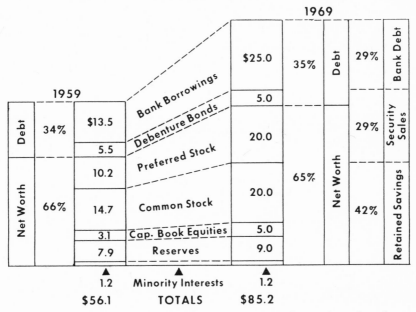

In its 1959 financial plan, Southern States projected capital needs and sources for ten years. This chart shows an anticipated increase in total capital from $56.1 million to $85.2 million, and the planned changes in the composition of these totals.

An excellent illustration of financial planning by one of the larger farmer cooperatives (Southern States Cooperative, Inc.) and the answers which it developed regarding net worth and other capital requirements, is available in two published articles by officers of the association.[5] As reported in these articles, the cooperative had experienced satisfactory growth beginning with $11,000 of paid-in capital or net worth in 1923 and expanding to $56.1 million of assets by 1959, with 66 percent ($37.1

---

[5] F. M. Armbrecht, "Financial Planning, A Case Study—Southern States Cooperative, Inc.," *American Cooperation 1959,* pp. 44-8; and W. T. Steele, Jr., "Financing—How We Do It in Southern States," *American Cooperation 1961,* pp. 64-9.

million) of the latter amount being net worth and the balance borrowed funds. Questions were raised, however, as to whether the financing plan which had been followed was the best one for the cooperative, considering the nature and expected rate of future development and growth. A special question was whether there should be some revamping of the

FIGURE 3

Planned Sources of New Capital, 1959-1969
Southern States Cooperative, Inc. 1959 Plan

FROM RETAINED NET SAVINGS	**$15.3**	$8.3	Additional
		7.0	Replacement
FROM SALE OF SECURITIES - Preferred Stock Debentures	19.8	9.3	Additional
		10.5	Replacement
FROM BANK BORROWINGS	25.0	11.5	Additional
		13.5	Replacement

As shown in Figure 2, Southern States anticipated in its 1959 plan a ten-year increase in total capital requirements of $29.1 million. This chart shows how it planned to obtain not only this additional capital but also sources of required replacement estimated to total $31.0 million.

sources of capital. A firm of investment bankers was employed to assist in studying these problems and in developing a financial plan for the succeeding ten years.

Full details of this planning operation are not needed for this discussion. Those dealing with the estimation of the amounts, types, and sources of required capital, however, are of particular interest. Figure 2 shows the projection from 1959 to 1969 of total capital requirements and the changes in types and sources. It will be noted that total capital was expected to increase from $56.1 million to $85.2 million, an increase of $29.1 million during the ten-year period. It was planned that of the $85.2 million needed in 1969, 65 percent would be furnished by net worth and 35 percent by the issuance of debenture bonds and bank borrowings. Figure 3 presents the manner in which capital would be raised during the ten-year period. A total of $60.1 million was expected to be needed of which $31.0 million would be replacement capital and $29.1 million would represent new funds.

These excerpts from Southern States' experience illustrate how financial planning develops answers to questions about capital requirements, the relative amounts to be furnished by net worth and borrowings, and other aspects of the net worth or equity capital problems. The answers which Southern States got from its planning are not necessarily applicable to other cooperatives. As has been stated, each association has its own set of circumstances, problems, and objectives which must be considered when making the financial plan and arriving at answers that will be applicable to that particular organization's operations.

In making financial plans, it must be recognized that future developments cannot always be foreseen, and the plan may not work out as projected. This happened to be the case with the Southern States 1959 plan. Because of unanticipated changes in operations, total capital needs did not increase as projected in Figures 2 and 3. Bank borrowing and other phases of the financial plan were adjusted as the new trends of operations and capital needs became more clear.

Inability to forecast future conditions and operations accurately does not mean, however, that financial planning is without value. Every business has to look ahead and make preliminary decisions regarding future operations, expansions or contractions. Even normal operations require capital, and provisions must be made for the needed funds. As was done by Southern States, adaptations to unexpected developments can be made quickly and smoothly if a basic financial plan has been prepared. Furthermore, if borrowed funds will be needed or increased because of the changed situation, a lender is likely to have a more favorable attitude if the applicant cooperative has a basic financial plan which can readily be revised.

Factors Affecting Amount of Net Worth Needed

As previously stated, there is no single formula which can be universally applied in determining the optimum proportions of net worth and borrowed capital, but there are some considerations that have wide application and must enter into every financial plan. One of the most important of these is the relationship between the fixed charges (mainly the interest charges, but also principal maturities) accompanying the use of borrowed funds and the size and characteristics of the net income available for paying such charges. In the language of corporation finance this is referred to as the earnings-interest ratio, and in computing this ratio the greatest share of attention is usually given to the interest on bonds outstanding, since bonds are an especially important means of long-term corporate financing. In financial planning, however, the ratio involves interest on the entire debt structure as well as any fixed rate of dividend on preferred stock. Many corporations, and a few cooperatives, are using lease-back arrangements as a substitute for financing some types of fixed assets. In such cases, however, the rentals are fixed charges and properly should be included in the earnings-interest ratio computation.

In discussing the application of this principle to corporation finance, Burtchett and Hicks say "Theoretically, the limit to fixed charge securities is the amount of such securities upon which the earnings of the concern will pay interest and dividends and leave a sufficient residue for the common shares to cover their risks and investments." They also point out that repayment of the principal should be kept in mind when fixed-charge securities are issued.[6] Converting this language to terms applicable to farmer cooperatives it can be said that the residue of earnings after the fixed charges are paid should be adequate to provide some return on the investment which members have in the cooperative, in addition to providing reasonable patronage refunds.

Burtchett and Hicks also stress the point, previously made, that this residue after meeting the fixed charges, or the earnings-interest ratio, should be great enough to allow for the fluctuations of net income between good and bad years. They suggest that, while it is not necessarily correct for all cases, a rule which may be used as a preliminary guide is that "if the average earnings over several recent years are four times the amount of interest proposed on the entire debt structure, there is strong probability that in the future such interest will be earned."[7]

The most important factor determining whether four to one or some other ratio is adequate for a particular business is the likelihood of variability in the earnings residue. The relationship between the average degree of variability of net revenue and the type of capital structure is indicated in Table 9. While partly hypothetical this relationship is suggested by Burtchett and Hicks after observing the experience of many operating corporations. In short, the principle suggested by this discussion

---

[6] Floyd F. Burtchett and Clifford M. Hicks, *Corporation Finance* (3rd ed.; Johnsen Publishing Company, 1959), p. 260.
[7] *Ibid.*, p. 282.

and by the data in Table 9 is that as the risk of fluctuation of income increases the share of capital represented by non-interest bearing net worth should also increase.

TABLE 9

Theoretical Relationship Between Degree of Risk in Type of Business and Capital Structure

Degree of Risk in Operation	Degree of Fluctuation of Net Revenue[a]	Maximum Percentage of Financing by:		
		Mortgage bond	Preferred stock	Common stock
Very low	10	50	20	30
Low	15	40	25	35
Medium	20	30	30	40
Above average	25	15	30	55
High	30	—	30	70

Floyd M. Burtchett and Clifford M. Hicks, *Corporation Finance* (3rd ed.; Johnsen Publishing Company, 1959), p. 261.

[a] Average percentage by which the net revenues of one year would deviate from the net revenues of the year on either side of it, when computed over a period of not less than 10 years.

Among farmer cooperatives, the possibility of good and bad years must be taken into account in planning the capital structure. Fluctuations in net income may arise from poor crops, shifts in production patterns or consumer preferences, market price changes (including government price-support policy), competition, price wars, labor troubles, and general price-cost squeezes. Unfortunate management decisions also may have disastrous effects upon net income. The size of the net-worth cushion needed to protect against such contingencies must be carefully considered.

The type of operation likewise will affect net-worth requirements. Risks, and therefore required cushions, are normally higher in some cooperatives than in others. A marketing cooperative handling a product for which price changes can be hedged, or operating on a pool basis with a sound policy in making advances to growers, carries a minimum of risk. On the other hand, risks increase when there are more liberal policies in making unhedged advances to growers or in the case of supply cooperatives in selling on credit. Risks also are involved in inventory accumulations.

Net-worth requirements, furthermore, are related to the amount of investment in fixed assets which is necessary. A cooperative limiting its services to bargaining generally needs little net worth, because it requires no investment in plant or real estate, or even in inventory. But as real estate, processing plants, warehouses, and other fixed assets are accumulated, it is sound financing to have net worth keep pace with the increasing investment and, in addition, provide some excess for working capital. Under such circumstances, term borrowings which may be needed for further expansion usually can be secured by fixed assets.

Some of the considerations affecting the relative amounts of equity and other capital used may be illustrated by the following thumb-nail descriptions of the financing of seven types of cooperatives, selected at random:

Type of Cooperative	Assets (Percent)		Net Worth and Liabilities (Percent)	
Supply regional	Current	48	Current obligations	24
	Fixed (net)	42	Term debt	2
	Other	10	Net worth	74
		100		100

Net worth consists mainly of (a) retained patronage refunds in the form of preferred stock and (b) allocated reserve, revolved in accordance with capital needs at the directors' discretion. Fertilizer plant, feed mill, grain elevator, warehouses, and other fixed assets are fully covered by net worth, with an excess available for working capital. Most other capital needs are met by short-term borrowings.

Type of Cooperative	Assets (Percent)		Net Worth and Liabilities (Percent)	
Supply regional	Current	42	Current obligations	15
with marketing	Fixed (net)	54	Term debt	12
services	Other	4	Net worth	73
		100		100

Net worth is made up of equities retained after cash patronage payments. Retained equities are not revolved, but are considered as "permanent" capital. The purposes of term debt were to reduce seasonal borrowings and to finance expansion.

Type of Cooperative	Assets (Percent)		Net Worth and Liabilities (Percent)	
Citrus processing	Current	76	Current obligations	59
regional	Fixed (net)	20	Term debt	6
	Other	4	Net worth	35
		100		100

Aside from cash sales of qualifying common stock, net worth was built up by margins and capital retains, which are revolved. Net worth exceeds noncurrent assets and contributes to working capital. Current assets are mostly products being processed on a pool basis and are financed mainly

80

by members through delayed distribution of proceeds. With dependable market outlets, the relatively low net-worth ratio is adequate.

Type of Cooperative	Assets (Percent)		Net Worth and Liabilities (Percent)	
Cotton marketing	Current	86	Current obligations	78
regional	Fixed (net)	8	Term debt	5
	Other	6	Net worth	17
		100		100

Since the bulk of the assets consists of cotton inventory and storage receivables, with CCC loan privilege as a hedge, the main capital needs can be provided safely by short-term borrowings. The relatively small net worth is twice the amount of fixed assets. When inventories and receivables are at a seasonal low, net worth in relation to total assets is higher.

Type of Cooperative	Assets (Percent)		Net Worth and Liabilities (Percent)	
Dairy processing	Current	41	Current obligations	26
and marketing	Fixed (net)	51	Term debt	29
local	Other	8	Net worth	45
		100		100

Except for qualifying stock, equity capital is obtained by authorized deductions and revolved. Competitive pressure and the necessity for enlarging market outlets have forced continuous expansion and investment through acquisitions, mergers, modernization, and construction. This has strained the working capital position, made it difficult to keep up the revolving rate and required full use of credit. Recent policy has been to increase gradually the permanent capital in order to provide a better base for growth.

Type of Cooperative	Assets (Percent)		Net Worth and Liabilities (Percent)	
	(Large inventory, December 31)			
Seed purchasing	Current	92	Current obligations	88
and processing	Fixed (net)	6	Term debt	1
regional	Other	2	Net worth	11
		100		100
	(Small inventory, June 30)			
	Current	53	Current obligations	10
	Fixed (net)	39	Term debt	1
	Other	8	Net worth	89
		100		100

This case illustrates wide seasonal variation. Seeds are purchased and processed in fall and winter and distributed to members in the spring. The dependable market permits short-term financing with a small net worth.

Type of Cooperative	Assets (Percent)		Net Worth and Liabilities (Percent)	
34 tobacco marketing	Current	97	Current obligations	96
associations. (Aver-	Fixed (net)	2	Term debt	—
ages from 1962 sur-	Other	1	Net worth	4
vey by FCS)		100		100

With 100 percent financing of inventories through CCC loans, net worth is needed only for providing fixed and miscellaneous assets.

The main point illustrated by these actual cases is that the method of financing, and particularly the relative amount of net worth needed, varies with—and should be adapted to—the type of operation, the character of the risks and numerous other considerations. The 50 percent ratio of net worth to total assets, often thought to be a standard requirement by lenders, is fairly accurate as a preliminary guideline. But most cooperatives have more net worth than this, except perhaps during seasonal peaks of short-term borrowing, while some operate successfully on less. The important principle is that the optimum amount should be carefully worked out in a financial plan which takes account of these considerations and then projects the elements and stability of the cash flow and the related types and amounts of capital needs.[8]

Methods of Building Net Worth

Each cooperative likewise must determine which methods and policies for building net worth are best suited to its particular circumstances. As will be noted from Table 10, by far the most important source of equity capital for farmer cooperatives, shown by the 1954 survey, is some form of deduction from gross sales proceeds or retains from net income. In the case of the marketing cooperatives, referring to the combined totals for locals and regionals, 18.05 percent came from authorized deductions from sales proceeds, while 58.8 percent came from patronage refunds withheld, making a total of 76.85 from withholdings in some form. In addition, there were some such withholdings in combination with purchase arrangements. Purchase of stock by members, and perhaps by some outsiders, in itself provided only 8.99 percent, with some additional proceeds derived from the combinations referred to above.

---

[8] For further illustrations of the variations in the relative amount of net worth in the capital structure of marketing cooperatives handling different products, see Hulbert, Griffin, and Gardner, *op. cit.*, pp. 6-7.

In the case of farm supply cooperatives, again referring to the combined figures for locals and regionals, there were, of course, no authorized deductions from proceeds of products sold for members, but patronage refunds retained accounted for 63.3 percent, with some additional amounts in the combinations with purchases of stock and certificates. The local farm supply cooperatives appear to depend somewhat more on retaining refunds than do the regionals.

TABLE 10

Methods of Acquiring Equity Capital of Marketing and Farm Supply Cooperatives, Fiscal Year 1954

(In Percent)

Type of Association	Purchase	Author-ized Deduc-tions	Refunds Retained	Purchase, and Refunds Retained	Purchase, Authorized Deductions and Refunds Retained	Total
Marketing						
Locals and						
regionals	8.99	18.05	58.80	9.27	4.89	100.00
Locals	7.88	14.75	66.11	7.68	3.58	100.00
Regionals	9.32	19.01	56.66	9.74	5.27	100.00
Farm Supply						
Locals and						
regionals	23.43	—	63.30	8.56	4.71	100.00
Locals	16.89	—	66.21	15.48	1.42	100.00
Regionals	24.37	—	62.88	7.57	5.18	100.00
Marketing and						
Farm Supply						
Locals and						
regionals	15.27	10.47	60.75	8.96	4.55	100.00
Locals	10.57	10.59	66.14	10.01	2.69	100.00
Regionals	16.31	10.44	59.55	8.73	4.97	100.00

Helim H. Hulbert, Nelda Griffin, and Kelsey B. Gardner, *Methods of Financing Farmer Cooperatives*, Farmer Cooperative Service, General Report 32, June 1957. Adapted from Figure 4.

The 1954 survey also revealed that there were a variety of ways in which the components shown in Table 8 were accumulated. These variations have been summarized in Table 11.

The information in Tables 10 and 11 regarding the methods by which farmer cooperatives acquire or build equity capital is consistent with the patterns which were found in the lending experience of the banks for cooperatives summarized in Chapter Three, and also is similar to that of the business corporations referred to in Chapter Two. The usual pattern is that when a cooperative or other business first begins operations, the initial capital needed as a foundation is subscribed by members or, in the case of a non-cooperative business, by the proprietors. As for farmer cooperatives, if they are organized on a capital stock basis, the initial equity

TABLE 11

Methods of Acquiring Selected Components of Equity Capital of Marketing and Farm Supply Cooperatives, Fiscal Year 1954

(In Percent)

Method of Acquirement	Net Worth Item[a]			
	Common Stock	Preferred Stock	Certificates of Equity and Allocated Book Credits	Membership Voting Certificates
Purchase	26.14	39.11	3.30	54.21
Authorized deductions	2.47	1.67	20.27	10.72
Refunds retained	49.89	31.33	69.58	17.59
Purchase and authorized deductions	2.33	1.62	.45	13.86
Purchase and refunds retained	18.57	23.61	.46	3.52
Authorized deductions and refunds retained	.05	1.56	5.46	—
Purchase, authorized deductions and refunds retained	.55	1.10	.49	.10
Total	100.00	100.00	100.00	100.00
Percent of total equity capital	19.20	21.91	47.36	.22

Helim H. Hulbert, Nelda Griffin, and Kelsey B. Gardner, *Methods of Financing Farmer Cooperatives,* Farmer Cooperative Service, General Report 32, June 1957. Adapted from tables on pp. 17-21.
[a] Excludes unallocated reserves and miscellaneous accounts.

capital is obtained by selling common stock or a combination of common and preferred stock. If they are organized on a membership basis, the initial cash is obtained by selling memberships and perhaps certificates of equity.

As the cooperative gets under way, most subsequent additions to the initial capital subscriptions are obtained by retaining some part of the savings or, in the case of some marketing cooperatives, by deducting specified amounts from the proceeds of the sale of the products handled. These deductions or retains may be evidenced to the member in a variety of forms, including common stock, preferred stock, certificates of equity, or allocated book credits. Eventually there will be decisions as to whether, and when, any part of the deductions or retained savings should be revolved—that is, paid in cash to the owner at a later date. Occasionally, the certificates of equity which have been issued to represent deductions or patronage refunds will carry specified maturity dates. There is disagreement among the financial analysts as to whether, in that event, they should be regarded as a net worth item. An important fact for cooperative managements to consider, however, is that lenders generally will give less weight to such investments in evaluating the amount of cushion available in the financial structure to protect loans from risk of loss. While the building of the net worth account is achieved mainly by plowing back income or sales proceeds, some cooperatives find it desirable or necessary, especially in connection with expansion programs, to raise additional capital through the sale of some kind of stock or through the sale of other forms of equity interests.

As in the case of determining the amount of net worth needed, experience indicates that there is no single best way of accumulating equity capital or net worth. Each cooperative has its own separate problem and must decide which method or methods are best adapted to its circumstances and needs. The determination of the method is a part of the financial plan. Furthermore, there may be changes in circumstances which call for shifts in the method of capital accumulation. There will be further discussion of such possible shifts later in this chapter.

Is Net Worth Accumulation Becoming More Difficult?

The foregoing discussion has related to practices and problems of farmer cooperatives in accumulating net worth during recent and past years. Economic trends and legislative developments may make such problems more difficult in the future, or may at least result in some modification of policies or methods.

The opinions of cooperative leaders and workers regarding such prospective changes are significant. During the interviews conducted as a part of the study made for the banks for cooperatives, the equity capital problems of the cooperatives received a good deal of attention, and one of the frequently expressed views was that farmer cooperatives have greater difficulty in raising equity capital than do non-cooperative corporations. The main reason given was that the non-cooperative businesses have an advantage in being able to offer the incentive of capital gain on common stock sales. For this reason, there is usually a market for worthy corporation stocks. Furthermore, when such stock has been sold it becomes permanent capital for the issuing corporation, without any commitment as to retirement or an interest or dividend rate. Preferred stock, of course, may carry some such commitments. Cooperatives, on the other hand, are usually limited to their members in stock sales. There is no prospect for capital gains to offset the risk of impairment, and there is usually no loan or market value except at a discount, the rate of which depends on the record of the cooperative or on the prospect of its being able to carry on a program of revolving equities.

Another view frequently expressed was that whatever the disadvantages may have been in the past, farmer cooperatives may find the accumulation and maintenance of equity capital even more difficult in the future. Here again there were differences of opinion but the prevailing views emphasized the probable unfavorable effects of certain economic trends and legislation, especially those provisions of the Revenue Act of 1962 which deal with the Federal income tax status or requirements of cooperatives.

One unfavorable economic trend mentioned was that the rates of savings by cooperatives—the main sources of their net worth accumulations—are becoming smaller, especially at the local association level. The main reason given for the shrinking margins was increasing competition. In considering this point, it should be noted that there are wide variations in savings among commodities handled and among geographic areas. In some situations, savings are still at high levels. In other cases gross margins, even at the local level, have actually become wider because of more efficient operations by the regional, resulting in lower prices or charges to the local association. Nevertheless, net incomes of many local associations have shrunk because operating expenses have crept up to the point where they have offset the gains in gross margins. In some states, it was reported that savings at the local level have virtually disappeared and that the cash refunds made by the regional provide the only funds which can be distributed to farmer members.

A second fact cited as contributing to the net-worth problem was the urgent demand for capital on the farm. The necessity of expanding the scale of operations in order to survive calls for constantly-increasing investments in both operating capital and real estate. The rapid rise of such capital requirements is reflected in Table 12. As is true with averages generally, these figures do not show the high capitalization of the larger farms in the main producing areas. In the Corn Belt and other important areas, the total investment for the more efficient sizes of farms will range upward from $100,000, with many over $200,000. Such capital requirements, especially for the younger farmers who have not yet had time to accumulate a substantial net worth of their own, compete actively with the capital needs of the cooperative.

The situation just described, of course, is not a new one. For many years, farms have been consolidating, with the number of farms becoming fewer and the average size larger. The end of this trend is far from being in sight, and as technology advances further and the use of specialized

TABLE 12

Average Value of Production Assets Per Farm, Specified Years, 1940-1964

Year	Farm Real Estate	Non-Real Estate Assets	Total
1940	$ 4,608	$ 1,700	$ 6,308
1950	12,003	5,233	17,236
1960	32,480	9,820	42,300
1964	43,402	11,389	54,791

The Balance Sheet of Agriculture, 1964, U. S. Department of Agriculture, Information Bulletin 290, p. 15.

equipment becomes more extensive, the competition from the farm for capital not only will continue but may become more intensive.

Various solutions to these economic problems have been proposed by cooperative leaders. The most frequent comment made during the interviews was that the remedy rests largely with management. If there is an economic need and a real demand for the services of the cooperative, competent management can, according to this view, work out means of developing savings from which the needed capital can be retained. This means conducting operations in such a way that there will be sufficient earnings to permit some cash payments to patrons and some retention in the capital structure. In many instances, the solution for a struggling local association with little or no net income may be expansion of business volume through merger, consolidation, or acquisition in order to achieve cost reductions and support the level of management needed for successful growth.

Membership education was also stressed as a major solution. Farmers, especially the younger generation, must be shown that there are definite economic advantages to obtaining supplies and marketing their products the cooperative way. Data must be developed and presented in well-planned educational programs in order to convince members and potential members that it will be to their advantage to support the cooperative with investment as well as patronage. During the interviews an officer of one regional illustrated this point by stating that in his association's latest annual report the membership was informed that the annual dividend and patronage refund represented a 22 percent return on the total amount which farmers had invested in the affiliated local associations.[9] The effectiveness of such educational campaigns will depend upon the capability of the management and also upon the willingness of the board of directors and prominent members to assist in such campaigns.[10]

Permanent or Revolving Capital?

Another point emphasized by many cooperative leaders during the interviews was the need for having a substantial part of the capital structure in so-called "permanent" form. Although there was not full agreement on this subject, some cooperatives believe that the revolving fund is not a complete answer to the equity capital problem, and that often it is not adequate for maintaining sufficient net worth to support the investments required to keep pace with competition. There were frequent expressions of a need for a sizable permanent capital account on which there would be no commitments to revolve or pay specific dividend rates. Such capital would give the management more financial elbow room in which to operate and especially to finance growth.

These questions involve several basic policy issues regarding the sources and form of the net worth structure which have been receiving the attention of cooperative leaders. Farmer cooperatives generally are limited to two broad sources of equity capital: cash investments by members and some form of deductions or retains. Some cooperatives have tried, with varying degrees of success, to attract outside capital by the sale of some form of security to nonmembers. Obviously, the development of any such market depends upon the rate and dependability of return on the investment. One large dairy cooperative has established a good market for its preferred stock. Others have done fairly well with debenture bonds or certificates of indebtedness. Of these forms, only preferred stock can ordinarily be included as net worth, and few cooperatives have been able, or have even desired, to place substantial blocks of such stock in nonmem-

---

[9] While this information is not fully comparable, the USDA has estimated that in recent years the rate of return on all capital used in farm production has averaged as follows: 1961, 5.2 percent; 1962, 5.4 percent; 1963, 5.2 percent. See *The Balance Sheet of Agriculture, 1964*, U. S. Department of Agriculture, Information Bulletin 290, p. 15.

[10] For a good review of these issues see Glenn E. Heitz, *Will Farmers Invest Enough in Co-ops?*, Farm Credit Administration, Circular A-31, January 1961.

ber hands. Undoubtedly, efforts to attract outside capital will continue, but most cooperative leaders are convinced that the main reliance in building net worth must be upon member-patrons, either through purchase of securities with cash or by authorizing deductions from sales proceeds or retention of patronage refunds.

The practical problem faced by the management of a cooperative is how to build and maintain the amount of net worth needed for successful operation and growth and at the same time pay some return in cash on such investments to the owner of the equities or pay him the full principal amount of the equity in cash within a reasonable period of time. Under the revolving plan, when an association has accumulated the net worth which it requires, it pays off or retires in cash the oldest outstanding equities, using funds accumulated from the deductions or retains during the current year. In this manner, members in effect give the cooperative the free use of their equity investment during the period it is held by the association. Sometimes, of course, a return may be paid on this equity investment as a dividend or a rate of interest, depending partly on the form in which it is carried. Deductions or retains, as shown by Table 11, may be invested in common stock, preferred stock, certificates of equity, or book credit. Likewise, any part or the total amount of such accounts may be revolved.[11]

The revolving fund has been one of the principal methods of providing equity capital for farmer cooperatives. It has been used in a wide variety of forms and combinations, ranging from complete dependence upon a revolving plan through various combinations of revolving and permanent capital, to virtually complete dependence on permanent capital with no committed policy for systematic revolving. The so-called "permanent" capital normally is either common or preferred stock on which there is no commitment or policy as to revolving. Other permanent capital may be in the form of unallocated surplus or reserves.

Study of the available experience and information does not justify any overall conclusion that one particular combination of revolving and permanent capital is preferable to any other. Success stories can be found among cooperatives that have revolved all or nearly all of their capital regularly as earnings permitted, and they can also be found among those which have built up a net-worth structure composed principally of per-

---

[11] For a good description and analysis of the revolving fund method see Helim H. Hulbert, Nelda Griffin, and Kelsey B. Gardner, *Revolving Fund Method of Financing Farmer Cooperatives,* Farmer Cooperative Service, General Report 41, March 1958. This is a study of data obtained from 1157 marketing and farm supply cooperatives. See also Nelda Griffin, *How Adjustable Revolving Fund Capital Plan Works,* Farmer Cooperative Service, General Report 111, April 1963.

manent types of capital. Each has advantages and disadvantages which must be considered. Here again, the answer seems to be that the financial plan must be tailored to the circumstances and needs of the individual cooperative. There are some views, studies, and straws-in-the-wind, however, which are of interest in this connection and which may be taken into account in preparing the all-important financial plan for any cooperative.

One viewpoint is that the best capital structure should strike a balance between sources and kinds of funds. Glenn S. Fox, who was an officer of the Consumers Cooperative Association when he addressed the American Institute of Cooperation in 1961, suggested that the following allocation might represent a balanced financing program for Midwest cooperatives: (a) 25 percent of total assets in loans from banks for cooperatives (or other business creditors); (b) 25 percent in certificates of indebtedness, preferred shares, or loan capital—mainly from members, but representing cash investments; (c) 25 percent in deferred patronage refunds or a revolving fund; (d) 25 percent in foundation capital, such as common stock, memberships, patrons' equity reserves, and surplus. It will be noted that this proposed structure provides that 50 percent of the assets shall be represented by net worth, items (c) and (d), and that the net worth will be divided equally between a revolving fund and foundation, or permanent, capital. In his discussion regarding this concept of a balanced structure, Mr. Fox said that the Consumers Cooperative Association was at that time deficient in the foundation or permanent part of the structure but that financial plans provided for strengthening it.[12]

Other studies recommend greater emphasis on permanent capital and less dependence upon revolving funds than has been the prevailing practice for probably the majority of cooperatives in the past. An analysis of forty-four cooperative associations in Ohio covering changes in the financial structure from 1940-41 to 1960-61 indicated that during this period permanent capital as a percent of net worth tended to decline. After reviewing the past and prospective growth and the accompanying requirements of these cooperatives, the authors of the report on that analysis concluded that in meeting those needs "associations should attempt to make their existing and future capital as permanent as possible." As a guide they recommended a total capital structure such as that shown in Table 13.

In 1963, the National Milk Producers Federation employed a consulting firm to survey the principal methods of financing used by cooperatives and to review changes considered necessary in order to improve the financial

---

[12] "Financing For Growth And Strength," *American Cooperation 1961,* American Institute of Cooperation, pp. 51-8.

structure of dairy cooperatives. The unpublished report includes four recommendations pertinent to this discussion:

1. Requirement for permanent capitalization. The use of revolving funds as the principal source of equity capital is generally insufficient for dairy cooperatives which have a large percentage of investment in high cost, long life assets, such as buildings and equipment. Nonrevolving common stock and nonrevolving preferred stock should be used to a greater extent as permanently invested capital.

TABLE 13

Percentage Distribution of Total Capital of Agricultural Business Organizations That Transact Business Directly With Farmers

(In Percent)

Form of Capital	Stock Firms	Non-Stock Firms
Permanent capital	**60-75**	**40-50**
Common stocks or membership capital	40-45	20-25
Preferred stock	0-5	0
Earned surplus	20-25	20-25
Semi-permanent capital	**20-25**	**60-40**
Allocations	6-8	15-10
Reserves	5-7	20-15
Certificates without maturity dates	9-10	25-15
Non-permanent capital—Certificates and/or debenture bonds	**20-0**	**0-10**
Net worth (total capital)	**100.0**	**100.0**

G. F. Henning and Marshall Burkes, *Changes in the Financial Structure of Agricultural Business Organizations,* Ohio Agricultural Experiment Station, Research Bulletin 952, October 1963, p. 39.

2. Payment for the use of capital. In order to attract and retain capital from members, dividends should generally be paid for the use of capital when earned. This would pertain to both permanent capital in the form of capital stock and to some temporary capital represented by revolving funds.

3. Provision for capital accumulation. The continuing growth of cooperatives is accompanied by an increased requirement for permanent equity capital. A program should be established for securing these funds on a regular basis. This could be done by adopting a program for per unit deductions made on a monthly basis for subscriptions to capital stock.

4. Attraction of nonmember investment. Most dairy cooperatives still rely on the membership as the only source of equity capital. In the decade ahead, there will be greater need for dairy cooperatives to modify their policies in order to attract capital from nonmembers. This can be done by issuing nonvoting preferred stock or a separate class of common stock which would not endanger the operating control of the cooperative or let it pass into the hands of nonmembers.

An illustration of the applicability of at least a part of these recommendations was furnished by Leslie C. Mapp, general manager and treasurer of the Miami Valley Milk Producers Association, Dayton, Ohio, in an address to the American Institute of Cooperation in 1962. In connection with a review of the financing plan of the cooperative he stated:

> About 10 years ago we decided that it was not the wisest policy to have all of our capital on a revolving basis and at that time started issuing preferred stock which is non-revolving with members having the privilege of trading their certificates of indebtedness bearing 2½ percent interest for the non-revolving preferred stock bearing 4 percent dividends. Members also were encouraged to purchase preferred stock on a cash basis. As a result of this program during the last 10 years, today 50 percent of our capitalization is represented by non-revolving preferred stock and the other 50 percent by revolving certificates of indebtedness. This gives us a rather well-balanced program and through this system of capitalization we do not depend on savings to furnish the necessary capital for the organization. This system of capitalization also enables us to do advance planning, as we can project rather accurately the amount of capital that will be coming in for several years in advance."[13]

Effect of 1962 Revenue Act

While the foregoing references to studies, recommendations, and illustrations point to certain advantages in shifting the emphasis from revolving funds to more permanent types of net worth, there are numerous factors which will affect not only the method by which this may be done but even the desirability or practicability of such a shift in policy. Aside from the local circumstances affecting the individual cooperative, the relevant state laws and the possible necessity of modifying the bylaws of the association must be taken into account. Of special importance is the 1962 Revenue Act, which made important changes in the tax treatment of farmer cooperatives and their patrons and the tax reporting requirements applicable to such cooperatives.

---

[13] "How Miami Valley Milk Producers Association Plans For Tomorrow," *American Cooperation* 1962, p. 226.

It is not practicable, or even desirable, to describe the full effects of this law upon the policies which any individual association should follow in net worth accumulation. One reason such a discussion is not possible is that at the time of this writing the Internal Revenue Service has not yet issued all of the necessary regulations and interpretations. Another reason is that since many of the questions involve technical and legal points, every cooperative should have the benefit of competent counseling when adjusting its particular financial plan to these requirements.

Furthermore, there appears to be a difference of opinion among cooperative workers as to the nature of the impact of the 1962 act upon the operations of cooperatives and particularly upon the problem of net worth accumulation. This lack of agreement was indicated in a survey made by the Farmer Cooperative Service in 1963. The responses of cooperatives to the question indicated a wide variety of reactions, ranging all the way from the belief that the new requirements will result in a serious loss to members, to the suggestion that the requirements will inspire cooperative managements to give increased attention to the development of those services that will be of greatest benefit to the members and will provide them with the most significant economic returns.[14]

A recent study made at Oregon State University cites the 1962 Revenue Act as one factor that is likely to influence policies of cooperatives in building net worth. The following quotations from that report include other points that are of interest:

> The revolving fund procedure has provided a simple, sensible, and economic method of accumulating capital. However, the potential annual yield of new capital from this source may be reduced in the years ahead. The decline in net margins per dollar of sales and the change in the 1962 Revenue Act, which requires that 20% of net margin be paid in cash, are the two main reasons for reaching this conclusion. This study makes it clear that future capital requirements in growing firms are likely to be large. Incremental capital requirements in the future will occur in substantial "lumps" or blocks, and the timing of sources will be critical. Retained earnings may not be able to meet all of these requirements. . . .
>
> Alternatives suggested in this study consist primarily of increasing the use of common and/or preferred stock, in some cases, with some increased use of borrowed funds. To simply conclude that more and more common and preferred stock must be sold may be an unrealistic solution, since

---

[14] David Volkin, "Impact of 1962 Revenue Act on Cooperatives and Their Patrons." The Cooperative Accountant, Spring 1964, pp. 8-13. See also Raymond J. Mischler and David Volkin, How The Revenue Act of 1962 Affects Farmer Cooperatives, Farmer Cooperative Service, General Report 105, October 1962; Raymond J. Mischler, Handling Net Margins Under the New Tax Law, Farmer Cooperative Service, Information 39, June 1963.

it can be sold only in an environment of confidence, which many cooperatives find difficult to establish. However, if members were made aware of the need for invested capital and the benefits which would accrue to them as owners and patrons of a well-financed cooperative, they would be more inclined to support their association with both some invested funds and patronage. In this respect, member education is a vital part of any cooperative's overall financial program.[15]

Concluding Observations on Equity Capital

Without attempting a complete summary of the foregoing discussion of equity capital problems of farmer cooperatives, attention may be called to a few points that seem to stand out clearly.

1. The accumulation and maintenance of an adequate amount of equity capital or net worth is probably the most important phase of financing farmer cooperatives, partly because it is the foundation capital and therefore the basis for credit financing, and partly because of the numerous problems and possible variations in developing a satisfactory plan.

2. The amount of net worth needed, the form in which it should be built, and the methods of accumulating it should be worked out in a carefully prepared financial plan. In view of the numerous legal and practical complications, many cooperatives can benefit from competent counseling in the development of the plan.

3. Because of the endless variety of situations and conditions, no standardized formula for accumulation of net worth nor any optimum form of structure will have universal application. Each cooperative has its own problems and the plan must be adapted to each association.

4. There seem to be shifts in emphasis on methods of accumulating net worth and on the form of the structure. These shifts suggest a possible lessening of dependence upon the revolving fund and upon the retaining of patronage refunds, and putting greater emphasis upon permanent capital in the form of common or preferred stock which would be obtained through capital withholding or sale for cash. Whether or not such changing ideas should be recognized by any cooperative is again a question to be determined when working out the financial plan for the particular cooperative.

---

[15] Gerald E. Korzan and Edward L. Gray, *Capital for Growth and Adjustment of Agricultural Cooperatives,* Oregon State University, Station Bulletin 596, November 1964, pp. 4 and 31.

Chapter FIVE

Policies in Lending to Farmer Cooperatives

Having examined the role of equity capital or net worth in the financing of farmer cooperatives, the next consideration is the obtaining and use of borrowed capital. In some respects credit financing is easier and simpler, especially if there is a good foundation of net worth on which to build. At the same time, it is an extremely important phase of cooperative finance, because by using borrowed funds the scale of operations may be substantially enlarged, services to members improved, and general growth accelerated.

Use of Credit Gives Earnings Leverage

As an introduction to the discussion of the use of credit by farmer cooperatives, it may be helpful to review certain principles which are recognized in general corporation finance. The first is that net worth provides a basis by which a company can increase its earnings through the use of borrowed funds. In the language of corporation finance, this may be referred to as "trading on the equity," or as "leverage," since the equity capital enables a company to control additional amounts of capital and thus gives it increased power, or leverage. Such leverage is effective, however, only when the company has a rate of earnings on assets which exceeds the interest rate on the borrowed funds. The potential advantage of borrowing a portion of the total capital of the business when the overall

95

earning rate exceeds the rate of interest on the borrowed funds, is illustrated in a hypothetical situation in Table 14.

TABLE 14

Profits on $100,000 of Stock when $100,000 is Borrowed at 5 Percent Interest

Year	Earning Rate on Assets (In Percent)	Earnings	Interest	Earnings for Stock	Rate of Return on Stock (In Percent)
1	4	$ 8,000	$5,000	$ 3,000	3
2	6	12,000	5,000	7,000	7
3	7	14,000	5,000	9,000	9
4	8	16,000	5,000	11,000	11
5	2	4,000	5,000	ᵃ1,000	ᵃ1

Floyd F. Burtchett and Clifford M. Hicks, *Corporation Finance* (3rd ed.; Johnsen Publishing Company, 1959), p. 125. For a discussion of trading on the equity, see pp. 96 and 124-6 of this volume.
[a] Deficit.

This table not only illustrates the potential earnings leverage by trading on the equity, but also indicates that such financial management carries greater risk if there is a wide fluctuation in the overall rate of earnings on total assets. Furthermore, the higher the percentage of trading on equity, the greater the degree of risk assumed by the owners of the equity capital. There is also an increase in the risk taken by the lender.

The extent to which this leverage principle can be carried depends greatly on the stability of the operation conducted by the company. Where earnings are relatively stable, greater use can be made of borrowed funds in relation to net worth than can be done in industries that are highly competitive and unstable. This principle was illustrated in Table 9 in respect to the amount of net worth needed by a cooperative or other corporation. The effect upon capital structures of three different types of industries is further illustrated in Table 15. This table shows that public utilities, generally considered as having relatively stable incomes, include a substantially greater amount of long-term debt in their capital structure than do industrials, where a variety of factors contribute to wider fluctuations of income. Companies in the transportation business also use more long-term debt than industrials but not as much as public utilities.

These principles relating to the advantages and risks connected with the use of borrowed funds have virtually equal application to farmer cooperatives. There are differences, however, in the terms which should be used in expressing them. The purpose of cooperatives is not primarily to maximize earnings on common stock, but to provide services and maximize savings on business done for member patrons. Hence, credit should be used to supplement and give leverage to the owner-capital when it will

TABLE 15

Capital Structures of Companies in Three Types of Industries
(In Percent)

Item	Industrials	Public Utilities	Trans- portation
Current liabilities	7.5	8.0	6.0
Long-term debt	8.5	44.4	31.0
Preferred stock	1.5	10.3	4.0
Common stock	10.5	27.0	22.6
Surplus	22.0	9.0	33.0
Other liabilities	50.0	1.3	3.4
Total	100.0	100.0	100.0

Floyd M. Burtchett and Clifford M. Hicks, *Corporation Finance* (3rd ed.; Johnsen Publishing Company, 1959), p. 272.

enable the cooperative to conduct, enlarge or diversify operations in order to provide or increase needed services or to make or increase savings on services performed.

Loan Policy Discussion Relates Mainly to Banks for Cooperatives

In this discussion of the use of borrowed funds by farmer cooperatives, the banks for cooperatives will be the principal source of information regarding lending policies and practices and related problems. One compelling reason for this is that more data and other material are available regarding the operations of these banks than about those of any other major source of credit. The banks and their supervisory organization—the Cooperative Bank Service of the Farm Credit Administration—have assisted generously in providing information. These banks, moreover, were created specifically to make loans to farmers' marketing, supply, and business service cooperatives. They have become specialists in this type of financing and, as shown in Chapter Two, they are the major source of credit for such cooperatives. As principal lenders, they tend to set credit standards and in general set the pace of financing farmer cooperatives. A final point is that their lending policies and practices are of special interest to those cooperatives which are accumulating an investment in the capital stock of the banks.

The second most important source of borrowed funds for farmer cooperatives, as shown by the surveys, are individuals, most of whom are members of the cooperatives. Such indebtedness may be in several forms. It may be direct loans, evidenced by promissory notes. It may be in the form of certificates of indebtedness which are simply more formal and detailed statements that the cooperative owes money to the holder and agrees to pay a specified rate of interest and to make payment of the principal at a specified time. It should be recalled, in this connection, that in the discussion of net worth in Chapter Four, it was pointed out that certificates of indebtedness may be carried as equity capital, especially if they do not have a definite due date or a specified rate of interest. Sometimes notes and certificates of indebtedness are subordinated to other obligations. Still another form of such indebtedness is the debenture bond which, although not secured by specific collateral, includes provisions designed to strengthen the rights of the holder. It is of interest to note from Figure 2 that the Southern States Cooperative obtained part of its borrowed funds in this manner.

The obligations just discussed ordinarily are used by cooperatives to raise cash, but sometimes they are issued to defer a cash payment, as when a cooperative is liquidating the equity interest of a retiring or deceased member, refinancing an account payable, or making a partial settlement in cases of mergers or acquisitions. These obligations may be used also to evidence intercooperative lending. Cooperatives, both regionals and locals, lend to one another, either because of some emergency situation or because the lending cooperative may have surplus funds for investment. It will be recalled that there are also intercooperative equity investments.

In some respects, commercial banks are second in importance to the banks for cooperatives as sources of credit. Many local associations with a good record find it convenient to arrange for needed credit with a local bank which is close by and whose officers are friendly to the cooperative. Some regionals depend entirely upon commercial banks for credit. In other cases, borrowings may be split between banks for cooperatives and commercial banks. In view of the need for maintaining reasonable liquidity, some commercial banks are especially active in competing for the seasonal or commodity financing of well-established cooperatives.

Other miscellaneous sources, such as insurance companies and mutual funds or other investment funds, are of minor importance as credit sources. Federal government loans, other than those by the Commodity Credit Corporation and to electric and telephone cooperatives through the Rural Electrification Administration, while increasing are still relatively small in total.

Although the foregoing summaries describe the usual sources of credit, it should be noted that some farmer cooperatives are extensively involved in Commodity Credit Corporation loans. This is particularly true of tobacco marketing cooperatives which, in effect, finance inventories of members' products with Federal government credit designed as a price-support mechanism. Cotton, grain and other marketing cooperatives also take advantage of CCC credit to some extent. However, such loans are basically a price-support program and have definite limitations as a means of financing the normal operations and growth of farmers' marketing, supply, and business service cooperatives.

Sound Lending Policies Are Essential

As regards lending policies and practices, one of the first principles which must be observed by both the cooperative and the lender is that credit must be handled on a sound business basis. While elementary, this principle is as fundamental as that previously emphasized which asserts that farmer cooperatives are business organizations and must be run in a businesslike way. The importance of soundly-conceived programs for building equity capital has been stressed. The same attention must be given to the credit aspects at the time the financial plan is developed. Neither the lender nor the borrowing cooperative can afford to be careless in working out loan plans and agreements.

Organizations or persons that make a business of lending money can make profits only when they make loans on a basis where losses are held to a minimum. The banks for cooperatives are properly included in the professional classification. They are financial intermediaries which borrow funds from available sources, mainly on a wholesale basis, and lend them to others in amounts and on terms suited to their needs and at rates of interest somewhat higher than the cost of the funds loaned. Earnings are derived principally from the difference between the interest received and the interest paid.

Since they function in this manner, the lending practices of the banks for cooperatives must be as sound and the risks as carefully calculated as those of other professional lenders. It is recognized, of course, that the initial capital of the banks for cooperatives was furnished by the Federal government, and that this capital provided a substantial part of the loan funds used in the early operations. That stage, however, is well past. Loan funds now are obtained primarily from securities sold in the investment market, and the government capital is being rapidly replaced by equity investments of the farmer cooperatives which borrow from the banks.

While seeking to meet all reasonable credit needs which are on a sound basis, the banks for cooperatives have two special incentives to maintain a strong financial position. The first is to continue, and if possible, to strengthen, the favorable market for their debentures so that they may obtain loan funds at the lowest practicable costs and in the full amounts needed during all manner of business climate. The second incentive is to conduct the lending operations and loan servicing on an efficient basis so that the savings will accelerate the time when all government capital will be replaced by equities owned by the borrowing cooperatives, thereby permitting the revolving of these equities back to the owner-cooperatives. Closely related to these incentives, of course, is the need to maintain the value of the equities which the borrowing cooperatives have in the banks.

The overall record of the thirteen banks, over three decades of lending, indicates that their operations have been handled on a businesslike basis. From 1933, when they were organized, through June 30, 1964, loans made totaled $13.2 billion. Actual losses on loans charged off during this thirty-one year period totaled $5,081,447, or .04 percent of the total loans made. If the reserves for losses, amounting to $10,116,901 on that date, were added to the total losses actually charged off, the resulting total would be only .11 percent of the $13.2 billion of loans made. This record indicates that lending operations have been carried on in a very professional manner.

Closer examination of lending policies and practices, however, indicates that the banks have not been as conservative as the actual loss experience might suggest. During the period from 1933 to 1964, 6,274 cooperatives received loans from the banks. Actual losses were sustained on about 220 of these, or about 3.5 percent. Thus, while the total dollar amount of losses was relatively small, the number of cooperatives involving some loss was comparatively large. There were several individual cases, moreover, where losses were substantial, including one over $600,000, one over $400,000, two over $300,000, and nine between $100,000 and $300,000.

Neither the dollar losses actually charged off by the banks for cooperatives nor the number of cooperatives involved tells the complete story of the risks represented in the loans. Data in the banks' files indicate that for each dollar of bank losses, there have been several dollars of losses by members of the cooperatives. Such figures on losses by members, moreover, do not take into account the lack of earnings, the low returns on products handled, and similar losses which could not be estimated. Furthermore, the overall record of losses on loans does not reflect the risks represented in loans to cooperatives which became weakened for various reasons but were later restored to financial health, nor the risks taken in financing cooperatives on a low-equity basis.

Thus, while their overall record indicates that the banks for cooperatives have conducted their lending operations on a businesslike basis and have had good earnings and net worth accumulation, their experience shows that at the same time they have not been overcautious in their efforts to assist in the development of farmer cooperatives. They have frequently gone beyond conventional risk standards, either in helping a cooperative get started or in staying with it during time of trouble.

Some Lending Rules Set by Law and Regulations

The banks for cooperatives, like the other banks and associations which comprise the cooperative Farm Credit System, were established by an act of Congress and chartered by the Federal government. The enabling legislation and subsequent amendments not only gave the banks certain authorities but, in addition, prescribed some of the rules which must be observed in carrying out these authorities. The legislation provided further that the banks for cooperatives, like the other organizations in the Farm Credit System, would be supervised by the Farm Credit Administration, which was also authorized and was directed to supplement the statutory rules with appropriate regulations in certain areas of operation.[1]

Some of the rules prescribed by law and regulations under which the banks for cooperatives must operate are pertinent to this book. To be eligible to borrow from a bank for cooperatives, an association must be composed of and controlled by farmers; each member may have only one vote, or returns on equity investment must be limited to 8 percent; nonmember patronage must not exceed member patronage; and at least 90 percent of the voting media must be held by farmers or cooperatives eligible to borrow from the banks for cooperatives.

To such eligible cooperative associations, the banks for cooperatives offer a complete credit service. Lending limitations imposed by law are principally concerned with term loans for financing the acquisition, construction, expansion, or remodeling of facilities and equipment. These provisions deal mainly with security for the loan, length of term, and

---

[1] The enabling legislation and amendments are published in *Laws Administered By The Farm Credit Administration,* Farm Credit Administration, Circular 20 Revised, January 1957.

amortization, and thus far they have not seriously hampered the services of the banks. However, it is felt that the banks have developed thirty-two years of excellent experience in financing cooperatives, and that some cases warrant more flexibility than is possible under these legal limitations. It would seem in order, therefore, for the Farm Credit Administration to seek legislation that would permit it to substitute regulations for these statutory requirements. This action would make it easier to adapt the banks' services to the vast and rapid changes occurring in farmer cooperatives and enable them to give even more constructive service to the cooperatives they finance.

The law prescribes no comparable limitations on loans made by the banks for cooperatives to finance commodities or for operating capital, but certain requirements are included in the regulations of the Farm Credit Administration. In the case of loans to finance commodities, advances may be made on the security of practically any farm product or supply up to: (a) 75 percent of the value of unhedged (or 90 percent of the value of hedged) commodities covered by warehouse receipts; and (b) 65 percent of the value of unhedged (and 85 percent of the value of hedged) commodities covered by a first lien, such as a chattel mortgage or factor's lien. Such loans are generally made to finance advances or payments to growers for products delivered and for processing and marketing expenses.

Operating capital loans are made primarily to supplement the cooperative's net working capital, on either a seasonal or term basis. The seasonal loans may be used to finance inventories, for example, or the receivables arising from the sale of products handled. They may be secured or unsecured, depending upon the circumstances of each case. Term loans for operating capital are used to finance general operations over a longer period of time. They are usually secured by first mortgages on fixed assets, as in the case of facility loans.

While the law authorizes terms up to twenty years on facility loans, most term loans are made with shorter maturities, which are determined in consultation with representatives of the borrowing cooperative. These shorter maturities are a recognition of the highly specialized facilities and equipment that cooperatives use, involving rapid depreciation and obsolescence. Also influencing the maturity of such loans are changes in technology and the rapid shifts in the kinds of crops and livestock grown. It is not uncommon for term loans, prior to maturity, to be consolidated with new term credit and with revised repayment schedules. Such action extends the term of the original financing and may have the effect of providing a continuous loan balance outstanding as long as the affairs of the cooperative are conducted satisfactorily.

Regulations limit the size of a loan to a single borrower that may be retained by a single bank for cooperatives. Facility or operating loans, or a combination of such loans, to a single cooperative may not exceed 20 percent of the net worth of the bank. Commodity loans (excluding loans secured by Commodity Credit Corporation documents), or any combination of loans which includes commodity loans, may not exceed 35 percent of the net worth of the bank. Except for commodity or operating capital loans to finance commodities within the limits of government price support programs, total loans from the Central Bank for Cooperatives to any one farmer cooperative association may not exceed 25 percent of the net worth of the bank. Any exceptions to these rules must have the written approval of the Director of the Cooperative Bank Service of the Farm Credit Administration. When a cooperative needs a line of credit in excess of the lending limits so prescribed, either the Central Bank or another district bank, or a combination of such banks, may participate in the loan in a manner which will not exceed the lending limits of any one bank.

The basic loan documents for some large loans are referred to the director of the Cooperative Bank Service for advice and counsel prior to final approval by a bank for cooperatives. For certain other classes of loans specified by the regulations, loan papers are submitted for review after a loan is made.

How Loan Decisions Are Made

Other financial institutions which make loans to farmer cooperatives such as state and national banks and insurance companies, likewise are limited by statutory and supervisory requirements. In making loan decisions, therefore, the first requirement by professional lenders, including the banks for cooperatives, is recognition of the rules and regulations imposed by higher authorities. Within these boundaries, loan decisions are based upon the policy of the lending organization and the judgments of the credit administrators.

In the case of the banks for cooperatives, statutory and regulatory requirements are supplemented by certain policies or guidelines which have been developed over a period of years by the managements and the boards of directors. These are not uniform among the banks, nor are they rigid in their application. Exceptions are made when warranted by special circumstances. The nature of such individual bank policies may be illustrated by selected extracts from guideline statements prepared by several banks:

1. One bank's statement includes the following: With respect to equity capital, to be effective any business organization must continuously "look

ahead" and plan for its financial requirements. Where does it want to go, and how can it get there? This means planning for the immediate future, and planning for its longer term objectives.

This "looking ahead" includes a continuing appraisal of its objectives and of the resources required to accomplish those objectives. These include, of course, adequate plant and equipment and the "working assets" required to operate effectively. This continuous look ahead must also include the amount of capital required to finance total assets in use, and the present and future sources of such capital.

The basic source, of course, must be equity capital, supplied in a cooperative by members, stockholders, and patrons. Sometimes this is supplemented by long-term certificates of indebtedness, bonds, debentures, or similar securities evidencing funds loaned to the cooperative by its members and patrons for stated periods of time and often, but not always, subordinated to the rights of other creditors. The need to pay for investment capital and to revolve patronage capital on which no dividends or interest are paid, together with the necessity of being competitive in the overall cost of total capital in use, creates the need for a balanced source of equity capital—as between cost capital and free capital, a permanent type capital and revolving capital.

2. In connection with loans to finance facilities, another bank states that contractors' performance bonds are required for new construction. Three-year maintenance bonds are required on concrete elevator construction unless contractor is approved and provides at least a 10 percent carry-back for a period of three years. Contractors are discussed, but the bank does not recommend one contractor over another.

3. Another policy statement provides that loans for operating capital requirements are generally limited to: (a) $1.00 of loan funds for each dollar of the association's working capital when the loan is requested to supplement the permanent working capital requirement of the association, and (b) $2.00 of loan funds for each dollar of working capital when the loan is requested for seasonal requirements.

4. Another aspect of guidelines is illustrated by the following: Generally the bank uses three basic ratios in statement analysis. These ratios are (a) current, (b) fixed assets to net worth, and (c) total assets to net worth. The ratios, of and by themselves, are not considered by the bank as a conclusive test. These ratios are interpreted by weighing them with the figures and items behind the ratios and other statement relationships. As for example, in the current ratio it is desirable to have knowledge of the liquidity of the accounts receivable and inventories. It is also desirable to have knowledge of the sales-receivable relationship, the makeup of the inventory, and other significant relationships.

A thorough study of the operating statements of an applicant association reflects its growth or decline, as well as its operating efficiency, and provides an indication as to probable future results. In the case of marketing cooperatives that process the patron's products, the bank is interested in having knowledge of unit costs and unit returns to patrons. Also, these unit costs and results are compared with those of other organizations conducting similar types of operations.

The foregoing excerpts illustrate the nature of the guidelines developed by the individual banks. The receipt by a bank of the formal application for a loan commitment usually is preceded by informal discussions between representatives of the bank and the applicant cooperative. If the cooperative has not recently had a loan, and especially if it is a newly organized cooperative, the preliminary discussions may extend over a period of time. Sometimes changes in the bylaws are necessary to meet the legal eligibility requirements. Sometimes the bank may suggest changes in the financial structure or the operating plan. For established borrowers, the only discussion preceding submission of the formal application may be a telephone conversation.

The decision-making processes in the bank, following receipt of the formal application, include a thorough credit analysis, appraisal of plant and equipment if needed, and a certification regarding the eligibility of the association. The reports deal not only with the question of whether a loan should be made but also with requirements regarding collateral, insurance, custodian arrangements, terms, and so forth, that should be included in the loan agreement. The final decision on all these matters is made by the loan committee, which is composed of the bank's officers.

After they have evaluated all of the assembled information, the actual decision-making process by the loan committee members consists of the formation of judgments regarding the ability of the association to operate successfully, to use the credit for the benefit of its members, and to repay the loan with interest. These judgments have been sharpened by the extensive experience of the banks in financing specialized types of organizations. Frequently, when a new enterprise or an expensive new facility is to be financed, the bank will employ a competent consultant to advise it regarding the feasibility and prospects for success of the venture proposed by the cooperative. If the preliminary research and planning have been done by specialists who have the confidence of the bank, it may accept the research plans and cost estimates which have been developed by the association.

In a broad sense the fundamental considerations taken into account by the loan committee are those which the banks' experience has shown to be essential factors in the successful operation and growth of a farmer cooperative. In the evaluation process, the sizing up of the management, including the board of directors, is of major importance. The banks seek every available means of improving their skill in appraising this factor. Some useful ideas have been developed from research contracts between the American Management Association and Purdue University, North Carolina State University, and Oregon State University. A committee composed of secretaries of banks for cooperatives has developed a score sheet to help assess the various elements that make up effective management. When available, records of past performance, including various operating and financial ratios, are studied. Research carried on thus far has not developed practical ways of measuring management competence in quantitative terms. Consequently, these evaluations are almost always on a qualitative basis.[2]

Training activities undertaken by cooperatives and other organizations likewise have been helpful to bank analysts in evaluating the management capability of applicant associations. The programs of the American Institute of Cooperation and other cooperative gatherings invariably include panels, workshops, or other discussions on this subject. Management training institutes have been held under various sponsorships, including state and Federal extension workers, state cooperative councils, national cooperative organizations, and the banks for cooperatives. In some cases, professional management consulting firms have been employed to carry the main training load. Such has been the practice, for example, of the National Milk Producers Federation in its series of management institutes held for directors of affiliated cooperatives. One by-product of these activities has been the accumulation of a considerable body of training materials and general literature on cooperative management.[3]

---

[2] A management study of 48 country elevators in Iowa suggests the possibility of developing quantitative measures. See C. Phillip Baumel and Wayne A. Fuller, "Estimates of the Productivity of Management Practices in Local Agribusiness Firms," *Journal of Farm Economics,* November 1964, pp. 857-65. The authors conclude that while the evidence is not overwhelming "it does suggest that it is feasible to quantify non-numerical measures of management behavior and practices and to associate these measures with firm profitability." A further reference to the evaluation of management is made by Leo Garoian and Arnold F. Haseley, *The Board of Directors in Agricultural Marketing Business,* (Oregon State University, 1963), in Appendix D, "Appraising Management." This appendix includes a number of financial and operating ratios to be considered as well as a plan of analysis of operations, all of which was adapted from material developed by the American Institute of Management. In connection with the use of financial and operating ratios, an analysis of annual audits of 40 cooperatives in Ohio is reported by Marshall R. Burkes and George F. Henning, *Ratio Analysis Used to Measure Financial Strength of Agricultural Business Corporations,* Ohio Agricultural Experiment Station, A. E. 340, November 1963.

[3] Such publications, not previously cited, include an excellent manual by Milton L. Manuel, *Improving Management of Farmer Cooperatives,* Farmer Cooperative

It is significant to note also that the emphasis on management capability as an important factor in operating success and financing decisions is not confined to farmer cooperatives. Good management is well-recognized by general business administration authorities as the basic factor in the success of virtually all kinds of business. Its importance has been confirmed by numerous studies, such as the following one which summarizes a survey of the causes of general business failures in 1961:[4]

Reason for Failure		Frequency of Reason (In Percent)
Inexperience, incompetence		91.2
Inadequate sales	48.9	
Heavy operating expenses	6.5	
Receivables difficulties	10.3	
Inventory difficulties	7.4	
Excessive fixed assets	6.7	
Poor location	2.4	
Competitive weaknesses	21.3	
Other	3.1	
Neglect		3.0
Fraud		1.3
Disaster		0.9
Reasons unknown		3.6

Special Risk Factors Which Are Considered

While evaluation of management is important, there is a wide range of other factors that must be considered in the decision-making process. These include economic need, membership support, and the financial plan, in addition to overall management capability. The information regarding each of these is given careful attention and evaluated.

A detailed description of the decision process or an itemization of all the elements in its basic factors is not necessary for the purposes of this book. It will be of interest, however, to mention some items which have been frequent causes of trouble or which represent varying degrees of risk and therefore receive especially close attention.

In the case of marketing operations, financing policy and risk are likely to be related to the practice which the cooperative follows in making pay-

---

Service, General Report 120, June 1964. See also David Volkin and Nelda Griffin, *Management Training Among Farmer Cooperatives,* Farmer Cooperative Service, General Report 65, June 1959; and Kelsey B. Gardner, *Managing Farmer Cooperatives,* Farmer Cooperative Service, Educational Circular 17, November 1963.

[4] The data are from Dun and Bradstreet, Inc., and were included in Edward E. Reed, *Commercial Bank Management* (Harper and Row, Inc., 1963), p. 402.

ments or advances to patrons for products delivered to it for sale. In the first place, when there is protection from fluctuations in market prices through hedging—either in a futures market or by CCC loan privileges —risks are at a minimum. As already indicated, regulations permit maximum loans secured by stored commodities under such conditions, and the cooperative may safely make advances to patrons on the same basis. Risks are also minimized when marketing is handled on a pool basis and advances are made to members only as sales are made. Under this policy, there is little likelihood that advances to patrons will exceed the final net amount realized from sales.

There is greater risk in financing a marketing operation in which the cooperative purchases a product outright from the patron and acquires title to it. The risk in a merchandising service of this nature is that the market value of the product may fall before the cooperative disposes of it. The banks for cooperatives lend a smaller percentage of the market value in this type of operation and require the cooperative to own, or be able to borrow quickly, adequate amounts of working capital to protect the bank loan in the event of a severe drop in market prices. If the marketing operation includes some form of processing, such as freezing, canning, refining, or packaging, similar attention must be given to the policies of the cooperative with respect to inventory accumulations and sales programs.

A major risk in financing a cooperative which furnishes supplies arises in connection with selling on credit. Competitive conditions and customs in the community generally make it difficult to avoid some credit sales. Supply cooperatives therefore are urged to adopt firm, realistic accommodation credit policies, uniformly applied and enforced. The risk lies in using credit as a means of sales promotion or in drifting into a liberal credit policy because of management indecision, with the result that accounts receivable accumulate to a point where working capital is tied up and becomes unavailable for meeting regular operating requirements. In any case, credit sales should be made only in accordance with the credit policy established by the board of directors. Closely related to the receivables problem is the potential risk of inventory accumulation, with similar freezing of working capital.

Efforts have been made to keep credit sales to a minimum by encouraging patrons to obtain their own credit when necessary, so that they can pay cash for supplies. Some local supply cooperatives have developed working agreements with production credit associations or commercial banks for financing farmer members in this manner. Another approach has been for the regional cooperative to organize and capitalize a separate credit corporation which finances purchases that the local associations make from the regional. In some instances, the credit corporation finances farmer purchases directly. This method of financing sales also is watched closely by the banks for cooperatives, because of the possibility of using the credit corporation as a means of promoting sales through providing over-liberal credit.

For supply as well as for marketing operations, there is also a question as to whether the volume of business will be adequate to permit efficient, low-cost operations. Probably the best guarantee of volume support from the membership is an effective management which makes savings and cash returns to patrons. In many instances, however, especially when beginning a new enterprise, the cooperative enters into contracts with members, either to purchase a given amount of supplies for a specified number of years (applicable primarily when the members are other cooperatives) or in the case of marketing cooperatives, to deliver to the association the product from a specified number of acres over an agreed-upon period. In some instances, the loan agreements require such contracts with members to assure adequate volume.

Another situation that receives special attention from the credit analyst and the loan committee is that which arises when the financing involves the acquisition or construction of an expensive facility. There are several hazards in such a situation. One is the problem of whether management will have the necessary knowledge to handle the new operation effectively. Several cooperatives, for example, have gotten into trouble by undertaking to handle farm machinery with management that had not had previous experience with this kind of business under competitive conditions. Another hazard is whether the new venture is soundly conceived, from the standpoint of consumer demand and up-to-date technology. Sometimes plants have been built or acquired before the cooperative discovered that the equipment was already obsolete or that there was a poor market for the product. Still another hazard lies in obtaining accurate estimates and projections of construction costs and of operating costs and returns. There have been several instances in which a financial plan, including equity capital investments and loan commitments by the bank for cooperatives, was made on the basis of initial estimates and then, as construction proceeded, it was discovered that the estimates were seriously understated and that final costs would greatly exceed the financing originally contemplated. After commitments were made and construction started, however, the members and the lender had little choice but to see the project through and provide the additional funds required.

Some types of operations, because of their nature, carry higher risks than others. For example, in the overall experience of the banks for cooperatives, there has been no significant difference in loss experience between financing marketing operations and in financing supply operations. Since

1933, total loss as a percent of total loans made to finance marketing was .04 percent, while for supply financing it was .03 percent. In the marketing field, however, there have been some noticeable differences among commodities in loss experience. The highest rate has been for poultry and its products, with a total loss percentage of .25. Next have been fruits and vegetables with .09 percent, and dairy cooperatives with .08 percent. The lowest loss rates have been in financing grain, cotton, and certain other crops. The highest loss rates reflect, to some extent, a few large losses which were caused by unfortunate management decisions or drastic changes in the industry itself. The latter reason applies particularly to the poultry industry, where there have been tremendous shifts in both the geographic pattern and the organization and technology of production and marketing.

Although unfortunate loss experiences tend to make a lender wary when he is asked to finance similar operations, the banks for cooperatives do not arbitrarily eliminate any product or type of operation from their eligibility lists because of such experiences. They do try, however, to learn from such experiences and to double check the research, estimates, and projections so that further losses to the bank and to members of the cooperatives will be minimized or avoided.

How Much Equity Capital Is Required?

The foregoing special considerations by no means comprise a complete list of the potential hazards to the organization or operation of a cooperative which are given special attention when its application for a loan is being studied. They are merely some of the more important problems which have developed during the banks' extensive lending experience and thus are points which receive closer scrutiny. Furthermore, they do not include one of the most important areas of risk—namely, financial structure and management. Since this area is really the end product of any financing program, it is appropriate that it should receive major attention by the credit analyst.

The first part of the financial plan to be examined is usually the net-worth structure: its size, composition, and sources. Problems, and to some extent policy, in this general area have already been discussed in Chapter Three, which dealt with the experience of the banks for cooperatives, and at greater length in Chapter Four, which was specifically concerned with equity capital problems. The discussion in these two chapters threw considerable light on requirements of the banks for cooperatives with respect to equity capital investments in financing a cooperative.

In restating the banks' position on these matters, it should first be noted that in general the banks believe that the borrowed funds should not exceed the net worth. This guideline has long been followed by conventional lenders in financing any type of business operation, cooperative and non-cooperative. Overall lending experience has justified such a requirement, as it is a protection both to the lender and to the owners of the business.

As has been indicated, however, the requirement is not an inflexible prerequisite to obtaining a loan from a bank for cooperatives. Some cooperatives, of course, as a matter of policy maintain a net worth that exceeds 50 percent of assets. On the other hand, the banks for cooperatives have financed a number of associations—both large and small, old and new—in which the members' equity investments were appreciably less than the conventional ratio. It has been noted that usually there were special circumstances in all such low-equity financing cases. These exceptional circumstances included situations in which the type of operation did not require the conventional amount of net worth, or in which other success factors were so unusually favorable that operations could be carried on satisfactorily and growth achieved with a smaller amount of foundation capital. In other instances, unforeseen disasters or miscalculations created a situation in which financing was continued although on a low-equity basis.

During the decision-making process, the closest attention is given to the financial structure and the financial plan of the cooperative, including its earning capacity and repayment ability. A major requirement is that the net worth accounts be adequate to meet the particular requirements for working capital and other needs which are required by the type of operations to be conducted. Thus the answer to the question as to what amount of net worth is needed cannot be given in fixed ratios, but must be made after study of the financial plan and requirements.

The emphasis placed by lenders upon adequate owner capital is further indicated by Table 16, which summarizes the reasons given by commercial banks for rejecting small business loan applications, as reported in a survey conducted by the Board of Governors of the Federal Reserve System. It will be noted that inadequate owner equity was the most-frequently cited reason for denying a loan application.

In addition to studying the adequacy of the net worth, the loan committee also considers its composition. One of the main concerns is whether there are fixed maturity dates, or fixed rates of revolvement or dividend rates, which would conflict with interest and principal payments to be made on the indebtedness of the cooperative. In evaluating the net-worth position of an applicant cooperative, the banks generally do not include with net worth any certificates of equity or other items which have definite maturity dates. The credit analyst will usually classify these as borrowed capital rather than equity capital, even though the holders may be members of the cooperative. The basic reasoning behind such a classification

TABLE 16

Relative Frequency of Reasons for Rejecting Small Business Loan Applications by Commercial Banks

(In Percent)

Type of Reason	Frequency for All Banks
Reasons involving credit worthiness of borrower:	
1. Not enough owner's equity in business	93
2. Poor earnings record	85
3. Questionable management ability	84
4. Collateral and insufficient quality	73
5. Slow and past due in trade or loan payments	69
6. Inadequacy of borrower's accounting system	51
7. New firm with no established earnings record	48
8. Poor moral risk	41
9. Other reasons	6
Reasons involving bank's overall policies:	
1. Reported maturity too long	71
2. Applicant has no established deposit relationship with bank	49
3. Applicant will not establish deposit relationship with bank	36
4. Type of loan not handled by bank	33
5. Line of business not handled by bank	21
6. Loan portfolio for type of loan already full	19
7. Other reasons	4
Reasons involving Federal or state banking laws or regulations:	
1. Loan too large for bank's legal loan limit	23
2. Other reasons	8

Board of Governors of the Federal Reserve System, *Financing Small Business,* Report to the Committee on Banking and Currency and the Select Committees on Small Business, parts I and II—Committee Print 1958, p. 415.

is that net worth should provide a cushion of capital that has no fixed maturity and should also provide a favorable relationship between fixed charges and net income.

This policy, too, is a flexible one, since the final decision depends on the soundness of the overall financial plan. There have been some instances in which all, or nearly all, of the so-called net worth of a cooperative consisted of certificates with definite maturity dates and in which the financial plan worked successfully and the cooperative prospered.

It is significant to note that during the study made for the banks for cooperatives, the cooperative leaders and workers interviewed expressed very little criticism of the policies being followed by the banks with respect to equity capital requirements. There was virtually no demand for more liberal lending policies, and the prevailing view was that even though the accumulation and maintenance of net worth are difficult, there should be no relaxing of standards.

Interest Rate Policy

The interest rates charged by each bank for cooperatives on loans made are determined by the board of directors of the bank, subject to approval by the Farm Credit Administration. Several basic factors are considered

Interest Rates on Debentures of Banks for Cooperatives and Other Money-Market Paper

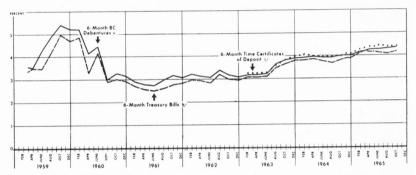

a Offering basis rate.

b Bond equivalent yield based on auction rate.

c Midpoint of range of secondary market offering rates for certificates of prime New York City banks.

Data provided by Farm Credit Administration. For comparable maturities, the interest cost of debentures sold by the banks for cooperatives is only slightly higher than that of United States securities and about the same as that of time certificates of deposit.

in this determination. The first is that the law provides that no rate shall be in excess of 6 percent. This law thus sets the maximum level.

The minimum level is that which is needed to provide enough income to cover the total cost of operating the banks. The total is made up of three classes of costs:

1. The cost of loanable funds. The principal source of such funds is debentures sold in the investment market, and the interest cost of funds

from this source is the major factor in determining the interest rates charged on loans. These debentures, classified as "agency" securities, are very favorably received in the market and can generally be sold on an interest yield basis which is only slightly above that of United States government securities having comparable maturities. This relationship, shown in Figure 4, reflects the reputation of the banks for cooperatives for making loans of high quality and for merchandising their debentures efficiently and effectively. These factors contribute greatly to the banks' ability to provide low-cost credit to their borrowers.

Debentures are usually issued about six times a year, in accordance with the banks' needs for funds. Maturities generally have been limited to six months or less. One reason for limiting such borrowings to relatively short terms is that interest rates in the wholesale market usually are lower for short-term than for intermediate- or long-term funds. However, since a substantial number of the loans made by the banks for cooperatives are for terms of one or more years, the question has been raised as to whether appropriate amounts of debentures sold in the market should not have terms that were related to the terms of the loans made. The policy decisions, thus far at least, have been to continue to borrow on a short-term basis as long as interest costs can be minimized in this manner and as long as money market conditions make it possible to refinance readily the short-term debentures and other borrowings as they mature. Another factor in this policy is that most term loans, in effect, can be made from funds represented by the net worth of the banks.

Funds obtained through the sale of debentures usually are supplemented by borrowings from commercial banks and from other Farm Credit banks (Federal land banks and Federal intermediate credit banks). There is also interbank borrowing among the banks for cooperatives. The interbank borrowings among banks in the Farm Credit System have been mutually advantageous and have increased significantly the efficient utilization of funds within the system.

Still another important source of loanable funds is the net worth of the banks for cooperatives, which has the effect of substantially reducing the average cost of loanable funds. The cost of such funds may be illustrated by data for the twelve months ended June 30, 1964. In that year, debenture sales totaled $1,126,000,000, at an average interest cost rate of 3.93 percent. Other borrowings were: $410 million from commercial banks, $215 million from Federal intermediate credit banks, $39 million from Federal land banks, and $156 million of borrowings among banks for ·cooperatives. Interest costs on such borrowings varied.

The extent to which net worth was used in providing loanable funds may be indicated roughly by noting that the average balance of loans outstanding during the year was $790.8 million, while the average balance of borrowings was $569 million. As a result of the use of substantial amounts of net-worth funds, the average net cost of all funds loaned was 2.73 percent. When compared with the 3.93 percent average cost of debentures sold, this rate illustrates one of the important benefits of a sizable net worth.

2. The operating expenses of the banks. This is another cost that must be paid from the income of the banks. It includes salaries, employee benefits, travel expenses, cost of space occupied, communication, advertising and public relations, bank examinations, supervisory expenses, and other miscellaneous expenses. The total expenses were .52 percent of the average loan balances outstanding during the year ended June 30, 1964.

3. Provision for losses. Appropriate amounts of income are carried to reserves so that losses can be absorbed, if and when they occur.

The total of these three classes of costs (interest charges on borrowed funds, bank operating expenses, and provision for losses) thus provides a guide to the minimum level of interest rates that should be charged on loans. There are at least two other factors which influence decisions regarding the specific level—somewhere between the minimum which has just been described and the statutory 6 percent maximum—at which interest rates on loans should be set.

1. The amount of margins or savings needed to carry out the financial plan of the bank is a major consideration. The financial plan includes estimates of the net worth needed to support anticipated growth of loan volume, as well as projections of the amounts of patronage refunds, the amounts of investments in Class C stock, and the amounts and final retirement date of all government capital (Class A stock). The goals set in these projections affect the level of interest rates needed to achieve the necessary savings.

Government capital, under present legislation, is retired annually in an amount equal to the amount of Class C stock invested in by borrowing cooperatives. Class C stock investments are made only by borrowing cooperatives, either by cash purchase in amounts equal to a stated percentage (between 10 and 25 percent) of the amounts of interest paid on the loans, or by distribution of patronage refunds from the bank's savings. Each borrowing cooperative, to be eligible to borrow, must own at least one share of Class C stock.

The cash purchase sometimes is erroneously confused with interest cost. Although it is added to, and related to, the interest payment, it actually is an investment in the common stock of the bank and cannot properly be considered an interest expense. Part of the banks' financial planning

115

includes determination of the rate of this so-called "override." At present it ranges from 10 to 20 percent among the banks.

When the total Class C stock investments in a bank reach a point permitting complete retirement of its government capital, the board of directors may consider revolving the Class C stock. Two of the banks reached this stage in 1965, and it is estimated that all banks will have retired their government capital not later than 1971. Such goals are considered in financial planning and in determining interest rate policy.[5]

When the revolving of Class C stock begins, both the cash and the patronage-refund investments will receive equal treatment. The revolving of the "override" stock will constitute a repayment of a cash investment. Any cash payments to borrowers originating from net margins or savings, whether the payments are made from the current year's patronage refunds or as part of the revolving program, will significantly reduce the net cost of loans to borrowers.

2. Competitive money market conditions are also taken into account by the board of directors in establishing interest rate policy. Some commercial banks actively seek certain cooperative loans, and such competition must be considered.

So far, however, it has not been the policy of the banks for cooperatives to negotiate special rates of interest with certain borrowers. All borrowers using any single bank have paid the same rate on the same type of loan. There usually are some differences in the rates for different types of loans. Well-secured loans to finance commodities in storage commonly carry a lower rate than term loans, for example.

The actual rates set by the board of directors of a bank thus are a synthesis of the considerations discussed above. They must not exceed the statutory limit; they must provide enough income to cover the cost of loanable funds, the bank's operating expenses, and provisions for losses; they must be adapted to the long-range financial plan of the bank; and they must recognize competitive conditions. The net result as of June 30, 1964, for example, showed variations among the thirteen banks from 4.25 to 5 percent for short-term and 4.5 to 5.5 percent for term loans. The

---

[5] At the time that all government capital is repaid, a bank for cooperatives becomes subject to the same Federal income tax requirements that are applicable to any corporation operating on a cooperative basis. The present law provides also that at that time the banks will no longer be required to pay a franchise tax to the government. This tax has constituted a payment to the government for the use of the funds it had invested in the banks (the Class A stock). The full tax burden, including taxes of the various states, cannot be readily estimated. Neither can the effect, if any, which such changes in the total tax position of the banks will have upon the interest rates they will charge on loans be determined at this time.

average rate received by the banks on all outstanding balances during the year was 4.87 percent.

Under interest rate policies followed thus far, loan volume has kept pace with the growth of capital needs of eligible cooperatives. At the same time, long-range plans regarding the net worth structures of the banks for cooperatives are being carried out on schedule. As cash payments are made to borrowers from patronage refunds and outstanding equity investments are revolved, the services to farmer cooperatives and the competitive position of the banks will be further improved.

Keeping Loan Policies Adjusted to Change

One of the important success factors for farmer cooperatives, revealed in the extensive lending experience of the banks for cooperatives, was not only the ability to meet an economic need but the ability to recognize that these needs change and to adapt operations and services to the changes. This principle applies with equal force to the banks for cooperatives themselves, not only because they are cooperatively organized but because they are business concerns whose survival and growth will depend on an adequate volume of business and on satisfactory income-expense margins. It is necessary, therefore, that the banks keep alert to the changing financing needs of farmer cooperatives and make appropriate adaptations in their lending policies and other services. Many such changes and adaptations, some of which required legislation, already have been made by the banks, and others are constantly under study. A number of suggestions about possible changes were made by cooperative leaders and workers interviewed during the study conducted for the banks.

In the interviews, there was some criticism of the policy of charging the same rate of interest to all borrowers on the same type of loan, regardless of differences in the size of the loan, the cost of servicing, or the degree of risk. Some of the cooperative leaders argued that the banks should have room for negotiating interest rates in order to compete on a better basis with other lenders. This issue has been discussed extensively over the years by Farm Credit directors and bank officers. The conclusion has been that the equal-rate-for-all-borrowers policy not only is more appropriate for a cooperative banking system but also has some definite advantages in administration. When surveyed on the question, moreover, the banks for cooperatives reported that present interest-rate policies are not a serious competitive disadvantage, and that only occasionally are loans lost to competitors because of the interest charges. In view of the differences of opinion regarding this aspect of interest-rate policy, however, it is likely that the question will be reopened from time to time.

During the interviews, the feeling also was expressed that the banks for cooperatives are inclined to give more attention to the larger loans and that applications from smaller cooperatives receive less encouragement. While it is the policy of the banks for cooperatives to serve all eligible credit-worthy cooperatives, it is possible that occasional comments may have created the impression just stated. One of the well-recognized facts of business life is that, other things being equal, the smaller business is at a disadvantage and is likely to have a harder fight for survival than the larger and more efficient operation. As pointed out in Chapter One, cooperative leaders are concerned about the need for combining many of the smaller and frequently competing cooperatives. The banks for cooperatives are often faced with decisions as to whether they should provide financing in situations where it clearly would be to the best interest of the farmers in the area if the cooperatives would merge or combine into a more effective organization. Banks for cooperatives do not have a fixed policy regarding such situations, and exercise their judgment regarding the procedure that is most beneficial to the farmers in the particular circumstances. Despite the advantages of the larger loans, it is a fact, as shown in Table 17 that many small loans are still made. As of June 30, 1964, one-sixth of all loans outstanding were for $10,000 or less, and 28 percent had balances of $25,000 or less.

While the data in Table 17 show that many relatively small loans are still being made, they also show that the size pattern of loans is changing in the same manner as the sizes of cooperatives themselves. The trend among farmer cooperatives, as among other types of businesses, is toward combining into fewer but larger (and usually stronger) associations. It is not unexpected, therefore, to note that during the ten years covered in Table 17 there was a substantial increase in the number and proportion of larger loans. Those with balances exceeding $1 million increased from 51 to 118 in number, while those with balances of $25,000 and less declined. The lending services of the banks for cooperatives therefore are being adjusted to larger credit requirements, including those of cooperatives which are entering the "big business" category. The banks have several lines of credit in excess of $60 million to cooperative organizations. Procedures for handling these larger individual credit lines have been developed by arranging participation with the Central Bank for Cooperatives and other district banks if needed.

Financial planning by the banks' managements also involves estimation of the rate at which the total amounts of loans made by the banks are likely to increase, and the net worths which will be needed to support the expected volume. The law provides that the capital stock of each bank shall be in such amount as the Farm Credit Administration determines to

TABLE 17

Number and Amount of Loans of Banks for Cooperatives Outstanding, June 30, 1954 and June 30, 1964, by Size[a]

Classification	Number of Borrowing Associations				Amount of Loans Outstanding			
	June 30, 1964		June 30, 1954		June 30, 1964		June 30, 1954	
	Number	Percent of Total	Number	Percent of Total	Amount (000 Omitted)	Percent of Total	Amount (000 Omitted)	Percent of Total
$10,00 and under	465	16.3	524	25.5	1,284	0.2	1,996	.7
$10,001 to $25,000	333	11.7	420	20.5	5,820	0.8	7,197	2.4
$25,001 to $50,000	459	16.1	393	19.2	17,033	2.2	14,269	4.7
$50,001 to $100,000	565	19.8	340	16.6	41,197	5.4	23,974	7.9
$100,001 to $300,000	670	23.4	247	12.0	113,216	14.9	39,990	13.1
$300,001 to $1,000,000	247	8.6	75	3.7	126,199	16.7	40,190	13.2
Over $1,000,000	118	4.1	51	2.5	452,715	59.8	176,349	58.0
Total	2,857	100.0	2,050	100.0	757,464	100.0	303,965	100.0

[a] Farm Credit Administration report prepared for use by the banks.

119

be required for the purpose of meeting the credit needs of eligible borrowers from the bank. The principal considerations in arriving at this decision are: (a) the amount of net worth needed in this type of operation in order to provide working capital and to provide a cushion of free capital which will be adequate to assure continued service in the event of emergency conditions; and (b) the ratio of owned to borrowed capital which should be maintained in order to assure the continued confidence of the investment market in the debentures issued by the banks. The board of directors of each bank decides what policies are to be followed in building or maintaining the required net worth structure. The capitalization required may to some extent, affect both the interest-rate policy and the amount of Class C stock investment that is related to the amount of interest paid by borrowers. More importantly, however, it will affect the rate at which the Class C stock can be revolved and the amount of patronage refunds which will be paid immediately in cash.

Another area in which adjustments to change eventually may be needed is in the definition of cooperatives eligible to borrow from the banks for cooperatives. As pointed out earlier, one of the statutory requirements of eligibility is that 90 percent of the voting media be held by farmers or by cooperatives eligible to borrow from the banks for cooperatives. It was pointed out also that as a result of the so-called urbanization of agriculture, farmer supply cooperatives are doing an increasing amount of business with nonfarmer patrons. Some cooperatives wish to encourage such patronage in order to maintain or build volume. To this end, they would like to see the 90 percent eligibility requirement reduced so that larger numbers of nonfarmer patrons could be taken in as members of the cooperative, although not to an extent which would permit nonfarmer members to gain control.

This may become a serious problem for some supply cooperatives serving areas where the number of bona fide farmers is diminishing and the number of rural nonfarmer residents is increasing. Suburban expansion and the location of industrial plants in the country are important factors contributing to this trend, illustrated in Figure 5. Thus far, efforts to relax the 90 percent eligibility requirement have not been successful. A considerable part of the opposition has come from marketing cooperatives which have not been affected unless they have expanded their services extensively into supply operations. One of the most notable effects of this trend has been upon the electric cooperatives, which in recent years have been adding large numbers of nonfarmer members.

Perhaps the most important areas requiring continuous critical scrutiny for possible need of adjustment to change is the structure of statutory and regulatory rules within which the banks for cooperatives must design

120

their financing programs for individual cooperatives. During the study made for the banks for cooperatives, a few association leaders expressed the feeling that the loan committees of the banks should have greater freedom in working out loan programs than is now permitted by these rules. Several persons questioned the advisability of the statutory limitation of twenty years on facility loans. There are additional factors which

FIGURE 5

Employment Status of the Rural Population

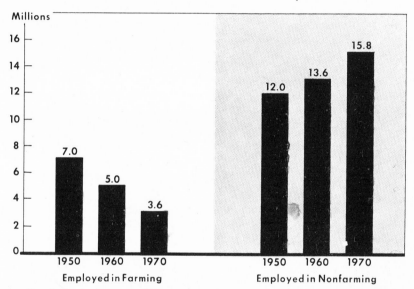

Based on data presented by John H. Southern, "Regional Growth and Development and Rural Areas," an address to the 42nd Annual Agricultural Outlook Conference, Washington, D. C., November 17, 1964. The shifting character of the rural population is projected to 1970.

suggest the desirability of critically examining these requirements, especially those which were established by Congress more than thirty years ago.

Of some significance in this connection is the practice by which many general business corporations obtain credit for terms in excess of ten and twenty years through the issuance of corporate bonds. Table 2 indicated that issuance of bonds is an important method of financing long-term needs. A separate study shows that most corporate bonds are issued for terms that are substantially longer than those of most facility loans made by the banks for cooperatives. The following data summarize a study of the maturity length, by ten-year periods, of all bond issues (excluding private placements) registered with the Securities and Exchange Commission from 1950 through 1961:[6]

Maturity Length (In Years)	Percent of all Bonds Issued	
	For Maturity Period	Cumulative
10 or less	4.36	4.36
11 - 20	32.94	37.30
21 - 30	52.30	89.30
31 - 40	9.79	99.39
Over 40	.61	100.00
Total	100.0	----

It will be noted that only 37 percent of the bonds had terms of twenty years or less, the maximum term permitted by law for facility loans by the banks for cooperatives. There were wide variations among industries in the average term. Some of those with the longest terms were: petroleum, refining, and related industries with an average term of 26.6 years; pipe-line transportation, with an average of 27.4 years; and electric, gas, and sanitary services with an average of 27.2 years. Communications also had a long average term, with 25.1 years. Even if the bonds from such industries were eliminated from the summary, almost 70 percent of the remaining bond issues fall within the eleven-year range between twenty and thirty years.

These figures suggest that as farmer cooperatives expand their activities and services into processing and manufacturing and grow in overall size, their needs may parallel those of non-cooperative corporations engaged in similar businesses and, as a considerable number of such corporations, they may find that longer term debt is appropriate for a part of their financial structure. A revision of maximum terms, and possibly of other requirements, would be particularly necessary if the banks for cooperatives should have the opportunity to finance electric and telephone cooperatives now financed by the Rural Electrification Administration. It is not inconceivable that such a situation might arise. If the banks for cooperatives should wish to pursue any such opportunity aggressively, a revision of lending policies would be necessary. Electric and other public utility financing generally is characterized not only by longer terms for funds borrowed but also by larger amounts of long-term borrowings in

---

[6] Condensed from a table in "How Many Years To Maturity," *Business Review,* Federal Reserve Bank of Philadelphia, February 1963. All of the bonds included in the study and in these data were issued by corporations of the United States, with the exception of a small volume of foreign government issues.

relation to net worth than have typified the financing of farmer marketing and purchasing cooperatives.

Aside from the specific considerations just mentioned, it seems doubtful that, as a continuing policy, lending rules set by Congress more than thirty years ago should be rigidly maintained regardless of changing times. Since the economy is not static, it should be possible to modify the rules freely if the needs of farmer cooperatives change. This problem has received the attention of the banks and the supervisory office, and adjustments in regulations can be and have been made.

In addition, as suggested earlier in this chapter, it would seem in order for the Farm Credit Administration to seek legislation that would permit it to substitute regulations for those statutory requirements that may limit full freedom of action. Such a change in the law, if enacted, would give the banks for cooperatives greater flexibility to adapt to changes in the credit needs of farmer cooperatives, if and when they occur.

Key Points Summarized

Restated briefly, the principal ideas developed in this chapter include the following:

1. A judicious use of borrowed funds to supplement net worth enables farmer cooperatives to enlarge and improve their services to members.

2. The banks for cooperatives provide more than one-half of the borrowed funds used by farmer cooperatives, with commercial banks and members also furnishing substantial amounts. Other sources include the Federal government and intercooperative lending.

3. The banks for cooperatives have become specialists in financing farmer cooperatives, and their objective is to keep lending services adapted to changing credit needs of cooperatives.

4. The debentures sold in the investment market are the principal source of loanable funds, and the cost of such funds is the major factor affecting interest rates charged on loans. Having an excellent market, these debentures should provide all the loanable funds needed in the foreseeable future, at interest costs only slightly above those of comparable United States government securities.

5. Other factors affecting interest rates charged on loans by the banks for cooperatives are: the statutory upper limit of 6 percent, operating expenses of the banks, provisions for losses, competitive conditions, and long-range financial plans, especially those involving the net-worth structure.

123

6. Stock investments made in the banks by borrowing cooperatives are expected to permit retirement of all government capital in the banks by about 1971. When borrowing cooperatives thus attain full ownership of a bank, it is expected that the bank will begin to revolve its borrower-owned (Class C) stock. Cash payments to borrowers from margins will reduce the interest cost paid on loans by borrowers.

7. Legislation has been suggested which will substitute supervisory regulations for laws pertaining to certain loan limitations. If enacted, the bank's ability to adapt lending operations to changing needs will be further improved.

Chapter SIX

Non-Lending Services to Cooperatives

It is common practice for business organizations engaged in lending money to assist customers—and sometimes potential customers—in more ways than simply the making of loans. While sometimes the assistance is of a personal nature (such as drafting simple wills or advising on investment problems), the service given most attention is that of making available the broad knowledge and business experience of the officers and loan specialists of the lending institution. Such counseling or advisory services have been developed by many of the more aggressive commercial and investment banks.

The primary aims in offering such assistance are to attract customers and to build and maintain the confidence and good will of the patrons of the lending institutions. Some of the large commercial banks maintain on their staffs specialists in various types of businesses whose professional skill is available to borrowers. One of these banks, for example, had advertised the way in which its specialists in financing the gas and oil industry helped a client develop a good-sized business, and has stated that the bank maintains eleven commercial divisions, each concentrating exclusively on one group of industries. Officers of smaller banks endeavor to become familiar with local industries and their related problems so that they can be helpful in advising customers connected with those industries.

The investment banker is an important source of advice and assistance in connection with longer-term financing. Where bond issues are under consideration, his knowledge of the market enables him to advise on the type of security and timing of sale, and he is likely to be sufficiently familiar with the industry involved so that he can form intelligent judgments regarding the desirability of the investment or operation to be financed. Because of their wide range of acquaintances, investment bankers sometimes can give advice regarding other companies which might be available for merger or acquisition, and in such cases they can act also as evaluation experts and negotiators and can give other assistance in working out the consolidation.

Other financing intermediaries organized to provide specialized types of credit, such as financing inventories or refinancing sales contracts, may provide expert counseling on related business problems. Generally, such counseling services by professional lenders contribute to loan servicing by improving the confidential borrower-lender relationship in addition to attracting and holding customers.

Banks for Cooperatives Designed for Specialized Services

When it comes to credit sources and related counseling assistance such as those just described, farmer cooperatives have an advantage over most other classes of business concerns. During the study made for the banks for cooperatives, a frequent comment by the persons interviewed was that although farmer cooperatives may sometimes be at a disadvantage in raising equity capital, they are more favorably situated in obtaining credit because then have access to virtually all of the same sources of credit as other businesses and also to the banks for cooperatives, which were specifically designed to finance and otherwise assist in the development of farmer cooperatives. These banks have been the leaders in financing farmer cooperatives, as was intended by the enabling legislation in the Farm Credit Act of 1933. In addition, however, they have gone considerably further than most other professional lenders in providing supplementary counseling and related types of assistance. Because of the circumstances connected with their origin and the specialized purpose for which they were created, the banks for cooperatives have more incentives than those of competing lenders to work with farmer cooperatives.

Some of these incentives stem from the heritage acquired by the banks for cooperatives from the Agricultural Marketing Act of 1929 and the policy directives given to the Federal Farm Board by Congress in that act. The 1929 legislation included the following language (12 USC 1141):

(a) It is declared to be the policy of Congress to promote the effective merchandising of agricultural commodities in interstate and foreign commerce so that the industry of agriculture will be placed on a basis of economic equality with other industries, and to that end to protect, control, and stabilize the currents of interstate and foreign commerce in the marketing of agricultural commodities and their food products—

. . .

(3) by encouraging the organization of producers into effective associations or corporations under their own control for greater unity of effort in marketing and by promoting the establishment and financing of a farm marketing system of producer-owned and producer-controlled cooperative associations and other agencies.

In the Executive Order of March 27, 1933, which transferred the powers and duties of the Federal Farm Board to the governor of the Farm Credit Administration, the foregoing expression of Congressional policy was retained. Thus the Federal statutes administered by the Farm Credit Administration, including subsequent amendments, still contain language which in effect directs the Farm Credit Administration to execute the powers vested in it "only in such manner as will, in the judgment of the Administration, aid to the fullest practicable extent in carrying out the policy above declared." [12 USC 1141, sec. 1(c)].

The language and the spirit of the Congressional policy statement in effect call for active assistance by the banks for cooperatives, not only in providing credit to farmer cooperatives but also in "promoting the establishment" of such organizations in order to place agriculture "on a basis of economic equality with other industries." Thus, the incentive and responsibilty to provide assistance to farmer cooperatives, which the other lenders do not have, originate from the fact that the banks received their initial capital from the revolving fund of the Federal Farm Board and that they also were charged with furthering some of the functions initially given to the Federal Farm Board. While the force of the original 1929 policy statement may have been weakened somewhat by the passage of time and by changes not anticipated, it is still recognized by the Farm Credit Administration which requires, as part of its supervisory authority, that all loans made by the banks for cooperatives must be in furtherance of the policy quoted above from the Agricultural Marketing Act of 1929.

Of more importance as incentives, undoubtedly, have been: that the only reason for the banks being brought into existence was to finance farmer cooperatives, that their growth and success have been directly dependent upon the growth and success of farmer cooperatives, and that eventually the banks will be completely owned by the cooperatives they serve.

Extensive Experience in Non-Lending Services

Aside from the circumstances just discussed, there are still others which have motivated the banks for cooperatives to counsel actively with farmer groups regarding the organization and financing of cooperatives and to advise them on many management and operating problems. These impelling conditions were the early difficulties and problems facing inexperienced farmers in developing effective business organizations, and the unfortunate efforts of those that did not succeed. It was clear to the leadership of the banks, from the very start of operations in 1933, that extensive assistance of this kind would be necessary before a sizable volume of loans to responsible borrowers could be built up.

A glimpse of some aspects of this situation was given in Chapter One, and particularly in Figure 1. The study from which the data in Figure 1 were obtained included additional information which throws some light on the problems facing the banks for cooperatives at the time of their organization.[1] This report summarized available data on farmer cooperative experience during the period 1875-1939. The statistics indicated that during that period 25,949 associations had been in existence, of which 14,655, or about 56 percent, had gone out of business by the end of 1939. The 11,000 or more cooperatives which had survived the trial-and-error period included many well-established and effective associations, some of which had been in business for as long as fifty years.

The financing assignment given to the banks for cooperatives in 1933 thus was not an easy one. While there was a nucleus of successful experience in operating and financing farmer cooperatives on which to build, the overall record indicated that the banks would be working in a high-risk field. In addition to the high mortality rate already mentioned, the Cochrane and Elsworth study showed that all but a small part of the discontinuances were involuntary, as follows:

Manner of Discontinuance	Percent
Forced out	95.4
Merged or consolidated	2.6
Sold at a profit	1.7
Reorganized	.3
Total	100.0

[1] W. W. Cochrane and R. H. Elsworth, *Farmers' Cooperative Discontinuances, 1875-1939*, Farm Credit Administration, Miscellaneous Report No. 65, June 1943.

The five reasons for discontinuance reported most often, and accounting for about 60 percent of the cases were in order of frequency: difficulties in the field of management, difficulties in the field of membership, natural or unavoidable causes, insufficient business for efficient operation, and financing and credit difficulties. A final significant fact is that, as indicated by Figure 1, the highest rates of discontinuance occurred during the ten years immediately preceding the organization of the banks for cooperatives.

In this setting, it was a matter of necessity for the banks to take an active part in working with farmer groups, not only to assure that sound loans were made, but also to help build cooperatives that could be financed and would thus furnish the loan volume needed for efficient bank operation. The banks' activities took several forms. Some of the established cooperatives could be financed with relatively little advisory help from the banks. As stated above, a considerable number had been in successful operation for a period of years and had established bases for credit. Some had received loans from the Federal Farm Board revolving fund, and a few had even been financed by commercial banks, although farmer cooperatives generally were not regarded as desirable credit risks by commercial banks at that time. From this nucleus of more substantial cooperatives came the initial loan volume of the banks for cooperatives.

Since there were relatively few loans for them to service, bank officers and staffs were able to spend substantial amounts of time working with cooperatives and with farmer groups interested in organizing cooperatives. Such activities included: participating in promotional or organizational meetings; assisting in forming new cooperatives where voids had been created by failures or where clear-cut needs existed; helping to draft bylaws and organizational details to meet eligibility or other requirements; counseling on fundamentals of success; advising on accounting systems and various phases of plans of operations; encouraging and even initiating needed mergers or consolidations; and taking an active part in developing the financial plans. After loans were closed, it was necessary to keep in constant touch with borrowing cooperatives in order to observe progress or to discover and help correct unfavorable trends before they had gone too far.

These promotional and loan-servicing activities contributed constructively to the maturing and growth of farmer cooperatives. There is little doubt that the counseling and leadership efforts of the banks, provided in connection with the financing of approximately 6,300 associations, have played an important part in the overall development of farmer cooperatives in the United States. This was particularly true in the first decade or so of the banks' operations. The experience also enabled bank officers and staff members to develop specialized skill in diagnosing trouble and in counseling on a wide variety of financing and operating problems.[2]

In more recent years, some changes have become apparent. As a by-product of the growth and maturing process, many cooperatives developed capable staffs and leadership of their own and therefore needed less assistance. Moreover, as regionals increased in size, influence, and resources, they began providing their affiliates with advisory services which formerly had been handled to some extent by the banks for cooperatives. When available, cooperatives also benefited from the services of specialists from land grant colleges, consulting firms, and similar sources.

As the need for advisory activities diminished, the banks were able to make necessary adjustments in the use of their resources. While promotional and counseling work was continued when required or requested, more bank manpower could be devoted to servicing the growing loan volume. Furthermore, with competition from other lenders increasing, greater consideration could be given to ways of effecting economies in operation and to the long-range programs of retiring government capital and beginning the revolving of member-borrower capital.

How Far Should Lender Counseling Go?

In view, on the one hand, of the nature of their origin, their specialized functions and ownership, and the undoubted benefits from past counseling and leadership services and, on the other, of the pressures to revolve equities in the banks, critical attention was given in the study made for the banks to the question of how far they should go in providing such supplementary services under present conditions. The wide range of opinions expressed by cooperative leaders and workers during the interviews indicates the difficult decisions in this area which constantly confront boards of directors and managements of the banks. On one point, however, there was virtually universal agreement. It was that the supplementary services provided to cooperatives by the banks in the past have been not

---

[2] This is an appropriate point at which to recognize the part played by the organization originally established in 1926 as the Division of Cooperative Marketing, USDA, and now known as the Farmer Cooperative Service, USDA. In 1929 it was transferred to the Federal Farm Board, and in 1933 it became the Cooperative Research and Service Division of the Farm Credit Administration. In 1953 it was given its present name and located in the USDA.

From the beginning, its research and advisory services have contributed greatly to the development of farmer cooperatives. From 1933 to 1953, as part of the Farm Credit Administration, it was particularly helpful to the banks for cooperatives in developing their relationships with cooperatives. Such assistance has continued since separation from the FCA as evidenced in part by the numerous citations of FCS publications and research throughout this book.

only helpful but necessary and should be continued. The divergence of opinions was on the *amount* of bank resources which should be devoted to such services.

One point of view expressed was that the activities of the banks in this area during the recent years have been at about the right level and should not be increased. It was believed to be more important now to divert additional earnings to build net worth, retire government capital, and make cash payments out of refunds to borrowers so that interest costs can be reduced. If a bank is too aggressive in urging changes or adoption of certain practices and policies it may be accused of meddling in matters which the board of directors and the management of the cooperative are competent to handle. In some of the stronger, larger regionals, the view was expressed that they are competently staffed and have the resources to handle such problems for both their own organization and their affiliated local and subsidiary associations. The banks for cooperatives, therefore, should confine their activities to lending money and should leave the advisory field to the regionals. Another reason given in a few instances was that some of the banks for cooperatives, being relatively small institutions and limited to the credit function, have difficulty obtaining personnel with special technical competence equal to that of the large "big business" cooperatives which are concerned with a wider range of operations.

In total number, the foregoing attitudes represented the minority view. Most of those expressing opinions on the subject thought that there was a need for expanding such services by the banks. They said that although there has been great improvement in the management capability of most cooperatives, there is still an extensive need for sound counseling and advisory assistance, especially to the smaller cooperatives. The availability of the Farmer Cooperative Service and, in some states, of extension workers, was recognized but was considered inadequate to do the entire job. Managers of other regionals said that their organizations did not have the resources to do the job, and that there was so much to be done in working with local affiliates that there was plenty of room for efforts by both the regional and the bank. They did emphasize, of course, that the services of the bank should be coordinated with those of the regional to avoid duplication of effort.

Quite a number of those interviewed emphasized the need of, and opportunity for, leadership by the banks. As far as need is concerned, one point made was that although there are a number of nationwide organizations of farmer cooperatives doing commendable work, there is a lack of concerted action in developing services along the most effective lines. Because of their major position in furnishing credit and counseling, the banks for cooperatives, it was argued, are already influential in guiding patterns of expansion and growth, but if they made it a more specific policy, they could be even more helpful, both in independent leadership and in working more actively with other cooperative groups. The implication of such views was that the power of the purse strings puts the banks in a favorable position to get things done.

In between the extreme viewpoints of minimum (and possibly reduced) non-lending services on the one hand and aggressive guidance and leadership on the other, there were many persons who believed that the banks must follow a middle-ground policy with a balanced allocation of resources divided among counseling, promotional, and leadership activities, while at the same time keeping operating costs at a level which would permit favorable and competitive rates of interest. In expressing such views, it was recognized that the banks would need to limit counseling services to those areas in which their personnel would be most competent. Counseling would center around financial planning and management, legal questions (particularly as they apply to eligibility to borrow), and tax and accounting problems, and would include participation in other activities and problems to the extent that the competence and size of staff would permit. It was recognized also that the banks would need to continue an active program in membership relations and business promotion.

Practical Problems in Providing Non-Lending Services

Most of the ideas and issues advanced during the interviews and summarized above have been considered by the boards of directors and the managements of the banks for cooperatives. Each bank has developed and carried out its own policies in these respects. As borrowing cooperatives acquire an ever-larger share in the banks, they are likely to take an increasing interest in the determination of the most effective means of providing these non-lending services. Subject to statutory and regulatory limitations and supervision, the owner-cooperatives should of course make the final decisions as to what services they wish from their banks.

The discussions with cooperative leaders and bank officers regarding these questions indicated that there are numerous practical problems involved in reaching policy-making decisions in this important area. One of the first requirements is effective two-way communication between the banks and their member-owner cooperatives. Membership support has long been recognized as one of the basic factors of cooperative success. Experience has demonstrated that in addition to providing satisfactory services, a cooperative must carry on a continuous educational program in

132

order to maintain the support of its members. The banks for cooperatives, being cooperatively organized themselves, have this same problem of membership relations. As government ownership fades from the picture, it will be increasingly important that the banks keep in close touch with their members, not only for the purpose of servicing outstanding loans, but also as part of an overall member-relations program and as a way of keeping informed about the views and wishes of their owners.

This problem has not been neglected by the banks. A great deal of spade work was done when they were building the initial volume of business and assisting generally in the development of the cooperative way of doing business. In recent years, attention has been given to more permanent forms of member- and public-relations activity. Annual reports and annual meetings of stockholders are a regular part of such programs. Several banks have established advisory committees with a rotated membership from cooperatives, well distributed geographically. These committees meet from time to time for the purpose of learning about the operations of the bank and, in turn, giving the bank their views on the problems of the cooperatives and their opinions regarding the bank's services. Such committees, of course, are only advisory, since policy decisions must be made by the boards of directors.

The managements of most of the banks for cooperatives believe that the most effective means of maintaining two-way communication with member-cooperatives is through frequent personal contacts. This is provided mainly through visits to the cooperatives by bank officers and staff members as often as the size of staff and workload permits. Such visits are mainly in connection with loan servicing, but they also permit exchange of information. Misunderstandings can be cleared up and mutual relationships improved more effectively through such personal visits than by correspondence or other means. Some banks supplement such contacts with regular newsletters.

The banks also take part in training sessions and other meetings organized by or for cooperatives to deal with general agricultural development in their districts. Members of the supervisory staff in the Farm Credit Administration likewise attend and participate in many such meetings, particularly those which have regional or nationwide representation.

The level of competence of the bank staff requires special consideration. Farmer cooperatives have been growing, and they will continue to grow in overall size and in complexity of operations. In the course of such growth the larger cooperatives, particularly, have developed management and administrative personnel whose competence and business sophistication are comparable to those of the larger successful general business corporations in the United States. It would seem reasonable to assume that banks which specialize in financing all kinds of cooperatives, including the larger associations, should have officers and staff members with stature and competence comparable to the upper-level personnel of the larger cooperatives in the district, so that they can evaluate financing programs intelligently and can assist effectively with financial planning and other counseling problems when called upon. One possible standard which boards of directors of banks for cooperatives might use when considering levels of competence for bank staffs would be the salary and competence levels of the management in the larger cooperatives being served in the district.

During the interview portion of the study made for the banks for cooperatives, officers in a few of the larger regional cooperatives raised a question as to whether the smaller banks could afford the salaries which such competence would require. In this connection, it has been pointed out that the boundaries of the original Farm Credit districts—which are also the boundaries of the territories served by the banks for cooperatives— and the locations of headquarters cities of the Farm Credit banks, including the banks for cooperatives, were determined in 1916-17. Since that time, there have been tremendous changes in the geography of agricultural production in the United States and the related pattern of cooperative development. One result is a wide variation among Farm Credit districts in the aggregate volume of agricultural output, the number of commercial farmers, the actual and potential volume of cooperative business, and the related size of the banks for cooperatives.

Mergers and consolidations of cooperatives, especially of the regional associations, are also affecting the locations of important cooperatives and the geography of cooperative financing. This fact has raised questions as to whether the locations of the banks for cooperatives, as well as the territories they serve and the pattern of their main offices and branches are adapted to giving the most effective service under the new and still-changing conditions. It was recognized by the few who raised such questions that any such reshaping of the present structure would be extremely difficult to carry out. It would disturb long-established relationships between the banks and operating cooperatives as well as with other units of the Farm Credit System. It would also involve the redistribution of equities and, perhaps most important, would require legislation. The possible benefits from any such reshaping certainly would need to be weighed carefully against the cost and difficulties of carrying out any such reorganization.

The questions raised in regard to the potential leadership role of the banks for cooperatives involve another area of policy-making decisions

134

on the part of both directors and managements of the banks and the Farm Credit Administration. There would appear to be little doubt that the loan decisions and related non-lending services and counseling which are connected with the granting of credits exceeding $1 billion a year have considerable influence in shaping the trends and patterns of development of farmer cooperatives. Only time will tell whether these trends are in the best interests of farmers and the public. How far, for example, should cooperatives go in centralizing and coordinating marketing of the various farm products, or in vertical integration of supply and marketing functions, or in the nationwide coordination and control of such activities as the procurement and manufacturing of raw materials for petroleum products, fertilizers, and mixed feeds? How rapidly should international trade by farmer cooperatives be pushed? Should export and import activities of the regionals be coordinated or should they be developed independently? What would be the optimum long-run relationships between farmer cooperatives and the consumer cooperatives? How far should farmer cooperatives go in acquiring control of retail outlets and in admitting non-farm patrons to membership?

These are some of the broad policy issues facing farmer cooperatives. Virtually all of them involve the use of credit. How active a role should these banks—which are the cooperatives' own credit system and their major source of credit—play, through the leverage of loan decisions and related counseling and guidance, in the development of answers to such questions and in the evolution of such major issues?

The potential influence of their broad lending power, and of the related counseling, guidance and leadership, presents risks as well as challenges to the directors and managements of the banks and to the supervisory officials in the Farm Credit Administration. One type of risk lies in the possibility that cooperatives or groups of cooperatives could use their banks to finance and promote unsound or questionable expansion of services and related investments. Such a risk would be somewhat comparable to that involved in using a captive credit corporation as a means of promoting sales. The possibility of using the banks in such a way may recall the time when some farm organization leaders resisted proposals to use the lending authorities in the Farm Credit System as incentives to farmers to participate in government farm programs.

While such possible risks should not be overlooked there appear to be adequate safeguards against using the banks for cooperatives as a means for promoting unsound projects. In the first place with their seasoned business judgment, the officers of the larger cooperatives would not be likely to favor any ventures which would risk their investments in the banks, the market for debentures, or their future usefulness by encouraging imprudent lending. A second hurdle is the board of directors of a bank. Under the present arrangements, cooperatives elect only two of the seven directors. This fact would make it difficult to work out an interlocking arrangement by which certain cooperative directors could also control or influence lending policy and decisions of one or more banks. Finally, the Farm Credit Administration can require that certain loans be submitted to it for counsel before they are closed, and it can define the type of loan which is to be pre-submitted. This general point, incidentally, underscores the importance of continuing Federal government supervision after retirement of all government capital.

In view of these safeguards, the challenges and responsibilities inherent in the potential influence of the banks for cooperatives' system would seem much more important than the possible risks. Whether done consciously or unconsciously, the loan decisions, the accompanying loan agreements, and the related conferences with cooperative officials undoubtedly have played—and will continue to play—a significant role in shaping the patterns of cooperative growth and development. There is little doubt that cooperative bank managements, boards of directors, and supervisory officials share with cooperative managements the responsibility for directing, or at least influencing, the development and growth of farmer cooperatives along the most effective lines.

This responsibility re-emphasizes the necessity for the bank directors and officers and the Farm Credit officials to keep in closest possible touch with cooperative development, with cooperative leaders, and with research and extension agencies concerned with farmer cooperatives. As previously emphasized, such contacts and communications must be on a two-way basis. Constant study and a smooth flow of information are prerequisites to the most effective use of these banks. One final point which must be mentioned is that the effectiveness of the banks for cooperatives depends also upon coordination among the thirteen banks themselves as to the policies and attitudes which are adopted or favored. This coordination is being accomplished through continuous conferences of Farm Credit directors and bank officers under the leadership of the Farm Credit Administration, including the immediate supervisory officials and the Federal Farm Credit Board.

Summary of Factors Related to Non-Lending Services

1. Since their organization, the banks for cooperatives have actively supplemented their lending functions with counseling on organization, management, and financial problems, with particular attention to the latter.

2. The incentives to assist cooperatives in this manner stem from: (a) special features in the historical background of the banks; (b) the banks' specialized function; and (c) the necessity to provide advisory service because of the generally low levels of management capability and financial status in farmer cooperatives which existed at the time that the banks began operations.

3. As needs diminished, these non-lending services tapered off somewhat. They will be continued indefinitely on a balanced basis, however, because there is still a demand and a need for them and because the banks' guidance and leadership influence are inseparable from their role as major lender. The full ownership of the banks by the borrowing cooperatives also will be a factor in the banks' future activities.

Chapter SEVEN

Do Farmer Cooperatives Need Additional Sources of Capital?

Farmer cooperatives have made substantial progress over the years and, through recent growth rates, have increased their share of the total volume of agricultural business. Nevertheless, not all cooperative leaders are content with these accomplishments. During the study made for the banks for cooperatives, a significant number of those interviewed expressed dissatisfaction with the overall progress which has been made. They were concerned about the relative positions of farmer cooperatives and non-cooperative agribusinesses, and felt that if cooperatives are to play an increasing role in placing farmers on a more equal footing with other economic groups and are to have a more effective voice in the market-place, they will need to become even larger and stronger.

Questions About Adequacy of Financing Arrangements

A variety of reasons were given for the alleged lag in the growth rates of farmer cooperatives. These included differences between farmer cooperatives and farm organizations in philosophy and objectives, competition rather than cooperation between cooperatives, uncertainty regarding economic needs because of competitive conditions, and lack of progressiveness and aggressiveness by cooperative managements. Some persons believed that inadequate financing facilities were a principal hindrance to more rapid growth and development. While financing inadequacies as a major handicap to growth represented a minority view, the number concerned about the question was sufficiently large to warrant an examination in this chapter of the general question of whether there is a need for supplementary sources of capital for farmer cooperatives.

There was considerable diversity of opinion on this subject. Some persons emphasized that the major difficulty usually is in the equity capital area, that there is no real shortage of credit, and that if a cooperative has an adequate net worth and its management and other factors are satisfactory, it will have no difficulty in obtaining whatever credit is needed. A few complained that the net worth and other requirements necessary to obtain loans from professional lenders (including the banks for cooperatives) were too stringent, and that more liberal lending policies would make it easier for cooperatives to obtain the capital needed for proposed expansion. Another relatively small group believed that there should be a sizable government fund available which could be used to finance extraordinary needs that might be beyond the capacity or credit policy of existing credit sources.

The various ideas expressed also included wide differences in attitudes toward the potential role of government. A few people felt that the Federal government was the only source which could furnish capital in the quantities and at the low cost which are needed. Most cooperative leaders, however, strongly opposed any substantial increase in the use of government funds, believing that along with credit would come increased government control. They felt that an enlarged program of government lending would be a reversal of the policy represented by the retirement of government capital from the banks for cooperatives. Their feeling was that the cooperatives should work out their own solutions to such problems and several possible efforts in that direction were mentioned, including improvements in the services of the banks for cooperatives, if and as required.

Most of these ideas have been voiced elsewhere from time to time by cooperative or farm organization people. For example, dissatisfaction with the growth rate of farmer cooperatives was expressed by Kenneth D. Naden, executive vice president of the National Council of Farmer Cooperatives, when he said to the board of directors of the National Live Stock Producers Association in March 1963 that "cooperatives are not growing fast enough to raise farmer bargaining power. They now handle about 15 percent of farm production supplies and about 25 percent of farm products marketed. These percentages have not increased greatly in recent years. This indicates we are just holding our own in terms of share of the market."[1]

Concern has also been expressed about the adequacy of present capital sources and the related effect upon the growth rate of cooperatives. For example, Senator (later Vice President) Hubert H. Humphrey, when introducing S. 2630, Food and Fiber Development Loan Act in 1961, stated that the financial resources needed by cooperatives cannot be provided other than through a lending operation conducted by the Federal government. Referring to Senator Humphrey's bill, Murray D. Lincoln, former president of the Nationwide Insurance Companies and member of the Federal Farm Credit Board, has stated: "This legislation holds forth a chance for survival for cooperatives and farmers while at the same time assuring reasonable prices for consumers. If farm operations and cooperatives are to survive, they must secure passage of this bill and of its provisions."[2]

In an address to the directors of the Cooperative League in January 1964, Clyde Ellis, general manager of the National Rural Electric Cooperative Association, proposed the establishment of a new government agency, to be called the Rural Cooperatives Administration, which would organize cooperatives so that they could undertake various activities that established firms do not consider sufficiently profitable, and would lend them the initial capital. In approving this idea, the directors of the Cooperative League proposed that the new agency not only lend money directly but be authorized also to insure loans made by the banks for cooperatives to new cooperatives.

While the ideas summarized above are not complete, they are sufficient to indicate a manifest degree of feeling that some additional source of capital, probably the Federal government, is needed to enable farmer cooperatives to keep pace with their competition and generally to add to their resources in order to contribute more toward improving the economic position of farmers. For the purpose of examining the various ideas regarding the need for supplementary capital, the proposals that have been made may be divided into three categories as follows:

1. Assistance in financing cooperatives, usually of a relatively small size, to be located in rural areas plagued with chronic underemployment and low incomes. In such instances local industries and markets are needed, but investment capital is very limited.

---

[1] As reported in *Washington Situation,* National Council of Farmer Cooperatives, March 29, 1963.

[2] *The Dividend,* October 26, 1961, published by Nationwide Insurance Companies.

140

2. At the opposite extreme, the establishment of a large pool of funds, probably furnished by the Federal government, which could be loaned to cooperatives to finance the purchase of large businesses or other rapid expansion of services in order to strengthen sharply the cooperatives' influence in both buying and selling.

3. Assistance in financing more normal cooperative development projects, which are generally intermediate in size between the first two mentioned. These projects appear to be justified by economic need but for some reason there is unusual difficulty in assembling enough equity capital to meet the operating needs and to provide a base for the necessary line of credit from conventional lenders.

These three types of proposals will be considered in the order in which they have just been mentioned.

Financing Cooperatives in Low-Income Areas

Beginning in the 1950's, the United States Department of Agriculture has given increased attention to those relatively large rural areas having chronically low incomes. The major price support programs administered by the department were of little benefit to farmers in such areas, as they had only small quantities of products to sell. Other approaches to rural development were explored. These activities were accelerated and implemented by the Area Redevelopment Act of 1961, which included provisions for loans, grants, technical help, and other assistance in certain areas designated because of underemployment or low income conditions. The agricultural phases of this program have been administered through the Office of Rural Areas Development of the Department of Agriculture. In order to assist in the establishment of cooperatives when such an approach seemed desirable, the act provided for loans to cooperatives which were unable to qualify for credit from a bank for cooperatives or other sources. Such loans may be made in amounts up to 65 percent of the cost of the facility or plant, with a repayment period of up to twenty-five years. No part of the proceeds of any such loan may be used for working capital. A number of loans have been made to farmer cooperatives under this act, some of which were reported to have been successful in attaining planned objectives.

The lending authorities of the Farmers Home Administration also have been increased by legislation, to facilitate certain types of cooperative development. Purchase of stock or other forms of investment in cooperatives was added to the purposes for which the FHA may make loans to farmers. The FHA was authorized to finance rural water systems and irrigation systems, housing for senior citizens and for farm laborers, the

141

use of land for community recreation areas, and cooperative action by family farmers in obtaining needed grazing resources.

The Economic Opportunity Act of 1964 added further authorities to FHA for the financing of rural cooperatives. Under this act, "FHA will help cooperatives formed by low-income farmers develop certain needed facilities that are not otherwise available. Among these are: storage, grading, washing, packing, freezing, and canning plants; sawmills; and slaughter houses. They will also help eligible cooperatives to: market agricultural products and handicraft items; purchase farm equipment, feed mixers, and farm supplies; and establish artificial breeding, trucking, and other services."[3]

The foregoing summary of recent steps to provide loans to cooperatives from government funds suggests several observations. In the first place, Congress apparently has been responsive to the views of those agricultural and cooperative leaders who believe that some form of government lending authority is needed to supplement existing sources of capital for cooperatives. The total amount which has been loaned thus far is comparatively small. In October 1964 it was stated the FHA had loaned more than $70 million to rural cooperatives in the past 3.5 years.[4]

One consistent feature of the authorities created so far has been to limit financing from these sources to cooperatives which are unable to obtain adequate credit at reasonable rates and terms from other sources, and to projects which have been determined to be economically feasible. This policy indicates that Congress does not wish the Federal government to embark on a financing program that will compete with or duplicate existing sources of credit for cooperatives.

A final observation is that these authorities provide financing for "rural" cooperatives. They are not restricted to cooperatives composed entirely, or even predominantly, of farmers, but may include both farm and nonfarm members. This feature broadens the area of potential service, and the inclusion of nonfarm people in the membership may cause a number of cooperatives which are ineligible to borrow from a bank for cooperatives to become interested in government credit.

"Giant Steps" Financing Proposals

The large-scale government fund type of proposal may be illustrated by the Food and Fiber Development Loan Act introduced by Senator

---

[3] *Helping Rural People Help Themselves—Through Cooperatives,* Farmer Cooperative Service, Information 46, October 1964, p. 15.

[4] *Ibid.*

Humphrey as S. 2630 in 1961. Senator Paul Douglas was a co-sponsor of the bill, and the plan had the active support of Murray Lincoln, former president of the Nationwide Insurance Companies, Clyde Ellis, general manager of the National Rural Electric Cooperative Association, and some others. The purpose of the bill was to create a government fund of up to $250 million from which loans could be made to farmer-consumer cooperatives to finance the purchase of grocery chains and related facilities. The objective was to set yardsticks in the market, for the benefit of both farmers and consumers. This proposal received very little attention in Congress, and only minor support from farmer cooperative leaders. Of the 119 cooperative leaders and workers interviewed during the study made for the banks for cooperatives, not more than half a dozen favored any such program.

Even though it is unlikely that Congress would approve such a plan, at least in the near future, there are several reasons why some attention should be given to it in a chapter devoted to consideration of the need for additional sources of capital for farmer cooperatives. One reason is that Congress, in the past, has on several occasions appropriated funds for making direct government loans to both individual farmers and their cooperatives. Loans to cooperatives have included, in addition to those discussed above, the revolving fund of the Federal Farm Board and the REA financing of electric and telephone cooperatives. Furthermore, direct government lending appeals to some people as a simple solution to economic difficulties, and for that reason it is likely to be proposed anew from time to time. Some recent developments could revive interest in large-scale government lending. One is exploration by several large farm organizations of the possibility of buying retail grocery chains, one of the central ideas in Senator Humphrey's Food and Fiber Development Loan Act. Purchase of large chains would require correspondingly large amounts of investment. Reactions to such investments by farmer cooperatives may be influenced, one way or another, by the results of the broad study of the food industry ordered by Congress in 1964.[5]

It is the success of the REA financing program, however, that may have stimulated a good part of the interest in the government-lending method of stimulating cooperative growth. This program has been cited as an example of the way in which cooperatives can be built up rapidly with the aid of low-cost credit from the Federal government. The validity of the REA experience as a demonstration of the idea that similar financing help

---

[5] This action established a 15-member National Commission on Food Marketing to make the study. Dr. George E. Brandow of Pennsylvania State University was named to head the research staff and $1.5 million was made available for the investigation.

for other types of farmer cooperatives under other conditions would be equally successful, should be closely examined.

The main features of this program are familiar to most cooperative workers. It has involved loans totaling more than $5 billion, made to more than 1,200 electric and telephone cooperatives in rural areas at a subsidized interest rate of 2 percent. When the first loans were made, most cooperatives were newly organized, and members were required to make only a nominal investment in the cooperative, usually about $5.00. Total capital requirements thus were furnished almost entirely by credit. Although many of these cooperatives operated on a deficit basis for a period, all but a few overcame their difficulties. The result of this financing operation, as of December 31, 1964, was 997 electric and 224 telephone cooperatives in operation, having total assets of more than $4 billion, REA (government) loans outstanding of about $3 billion, and a total net worth of about $900 million. There is little doubt that the resultant expansion and improvement of electric power and telephone services have been a major contribution to better living in rural areas. The issues raised by this experience which are of major significance at this time are: Would a similar government lending program for other types of farmer cooperatives be equally successful under present conditions, judged by both financial and welfare standards? Does the REA experience indicate that the amounts of equity capital normally considered necessary to meet operating requirements and to form a basis for conventional credit may be reduced?

Complete analysis and discussion of these issues would require more space than is available here. Comments, therefore, must be limited to what seem to be the most significant considerations. In evaluating the REA experience, one of the first features to be noted is that, except for the initial equity-capital requirements, the factors and circumstances generally considered essential to business success were extremely favorable. There were exceptions in some local situations, and they hampered the operations of the cooperatives serving those areas. In the aggregate, however, it is difficult to conceive a more favorable combination of circumstances. Briefly stated, the factors which compensated for the lack of equity capital and decreased the lending risks included the following:

1. A low interest rate (2 percent) reduced the fixed charges and contributed to wider operating margins.

2. Expansion of markets was faster than expected. Nonfarm rural customers contributed to this volume growth. Both the number of patrons and the consumption per customer increased more rapidly than had been anticipated.

3. Construction costs averaged less than were estimated.

144

4. Rates charged electric consumers were reduced, partly because of volume growth and partly because of reduced construction costs.

5. Stability of income, which is typical of utilities, helped reduce the risk normally connected with a small equity cushion. Utility financing generally depends less on equity capital and more on borrowed funds than do other industries. Both income stability and market expansion also were helped by the fact that the programs were born at the right time. The electric program started in 1936 near the bottom of a broad economic depression, and has operated during most of its life in a period of rising national income and agricultural improvement. Beginning in 1949, the telephone program also benefited from the postwar population growth and economic expansion. Another factor contributing to stability of income has been that once service has been installed, users tend to place both electric power and telephones high in their ranking of essential expenditures.

6. Effective management assistance and supervision by a government agency contributed materially to operating and financial success.

In summary, and in drawing limited conclusions regarding the two questions raised, it is difficult to visualize another large-scale government lending program to rural or farmer cooperatives in which there would be such an extremely favorable combination of success factors. The circumstances, for example, in the purchase of large nationwide grocery chains that has been proposed in connection with this type of government credit would be totally different. One major difference would be in the economic need and related growth potential. Electric and telephone services were either inadequate or nonexistent in rural areas, and the REA program was initiated under low-cost depression conditions. The retail and wholesale food industry, on the other hand, is already highly competitive and has no lack of facilities comparable to that which existed in rural electric and telephone services. Initial investments would be made on a high cost level. In view of the competitive conditions, the outlook for growth would be uncertain. Data available regarding profit margins raise questions as to what benefits could be added for consumers and, more important, for farmers through cooperative ownership of retail outlets. The study of the food industry which has been ordered by Congress should provide more reliable information concerning the possibility of making savings through cooperative ownership.

Special Equity Capital Financing

The interviews conducted during the earlier study indicated that the main interest in additional financing facilities was concerned with financing ventures having size levels somewhere between the two areas which have already been discussed. The typical situation cited usually involved a substantial investment which had a favorable economic outlook supported by careful research and expert opinion, but did not qualify for conventional financing because sufficient equity capital could not be raised. A number of examples were given in which a good opportunity was lost or at least delayed because of such equity capital difficulties. Questions raised by these instances were whether net worth requirements by conventional lenders were too high and whether it would be possible to develop some additional sources of equity capital so that conventional financing would be more readily available.

One of the cases frequently cited in connection with such questions was the purchase of the Welch Grape Juice Company by the National Grape Cooperative Association of Westfield, New York. As is widely known, Mr. G. M. Kaplan, who controlled all but a small number of shares of the original Welch Company, agreed to sell the company and its entire plant to the cooperative in 1952 under a purchase contract which provided for only a nominal down payment and terms which would permit payment of the total purchase price from earnings of the company over a period of twenty years.[6]

This case has received a great deal of attention because of its unusual but successful financing arrangements, which included the following features: a contract to purchase for $15 million a successful processing corporation, with virtually no down-payment; no net worth on the part of the purchasing cooperative except allocation certificates maturing in twenty years and arising from a 10 percent deduction from the price paid to growers for the grapes; sufficient earnings within five years to pay the original purchase price of $15 million, transfer title to the cooperative, and obtain conventional financing; and complete payment of all additional indebtedness out of earnings within two more years.

There is another part of this story, however, that is less well known. About four years before the 1952 purchase contract, Mr. Kaplan had offered to sell the Welch Company to the cooperative for $8 million. One requirement was that $3 million in cash would have to be raised by subscription from producers. It was expected that the remaining $5 million would be borrowed from conventional lenders. The campaign to raise member capital was not successful, and in July of 1949 the chairman of the board of directors of the cooperative announced that the proposed

---

[6] For additional details regarding this transaction see George W. Lamb, "The Welch Grape Juice Story" *American Cooperation 1954*, American Institute of Cooperation, p. 86. Additional information and progress reports appear in *News for Farmer Cooperatives*, Farmer Cooperative Service, September 1954, p. 16; November 1954, p. 5; February 1955, p. 16; April 1956, p. 2; October 1956, p. 3; November 1957; p. 22; and February 1960, p. 2.

purchase could not be completed.[7] In 1952, Mr. Kaplan made his second offer to sell to the growers, and was accepted.

Several features of the Welch transaction should be noted and evaluated with respect to their implications regarding methods of financing the purchase of a going concern or the acquisition of facilities by a cooperative having limited net worth resources. These points have a particular pertinence to the question of whether there is a need for additional sources of equity capital.

1. It should be noted, in the first place, that this purchase was financed by the vendor. Under such an arrangement, the vendor takes relatively little risk, since the contract permits him to reacquire the property without expensive foreclosure proceedings if the purchaser is unable to make the required payments. The extent of the purchaser's risk is that principal payments made on the contract would be lost if misfortune prevented completion of the contract. This method of financing has been used frequently by cooperatives and other businesses, as it permits expansion of facilities and operations with a minimum of equity capital.

It is very seldom, however, that a cooperative has as favorable an opportunity to purchase a successful business (including an established brand name) with no initial investment as did the association involved in the Welch transaction. "Shoestring" financing and expansion of this nature are possible when: (a) the owners of the business or facilities to be acquired are willing to sell on a purchase contract which calls for a very small down-payment; (b) the earnings from the enlarged operations produce enough funds to make the payments called for by the contract; (c) members of the cooperative are willing to enter into contracts to provide a volume of business sufficient to insure success of the operation; and (d) the outlook for the business continues sufficiently favorable so that conventional financing can be arranged when the unpaid balance of the contract has been reduced to the point at which title may be transferred from the vendor to the cooperative.

2. The success of the Welch transaction and of other purchase contracts which could be cited, does not necessarily demonstrate that conventional lenders should finance a large number of the proposals for low-equity expansion which cooperatives may submit to them. As was pointed out in Chapter Three, the extensive experience of the banks for cooperatives has shown that low-equity financing by conventional lenders should be undertaken only when all other success factors are extremely

---

[7] The July 30, 1949, issue of the Jamestown (N.Y.) *Sun* stated that the proposed $8 million purchase had failed because of an unsuccessful effort to raise $3 million by subscription from producers. The announcement was by Hall R. Clothier, chairman of the board of directors of the cooperative.

favorable. Such factors include capable management, good member support, an encouraging economic outlook, and sound financial planning. There is also some risk involved in the judgment and accuracy with which these factors are evaluated before the financing commitment is made.

In the Welch case there was an exceptionally favorable combination of these factors. Even with the good outlook which it had and with the benefit of hindsight, it would be rash to suggest financing the purchase of a $15 million business when the members of the cooperative made no cash investment whatever.

3. The experience with the first offer in the Welch case illustrates also that difficulty in raising the required amount of equity capital may sometimes prevent a cooperative from taking advantage of a favorable opportunity and thus may delay desirable expansion and growth. Such experiences are the basis for the view of some cooperative people that additional sources of equity capital would contribute to faster growth and development of farmer cooperatives.

The latter opinion was frequently expressed during the interviews in the study. A variety of viewpoints have been advanced regarding this problem and what, if anything, should be done about it. The prevailing attitude in the interviews was that it is a problem to be worked out in each individual case by the management and the members, with the counseling and other aid of any organizations or individuals that would be available. As has been stated, a frequent comment was that neither cooperatives nor the banks for cooperatives should relax their requirements with respect to appropriate amounts of foundation capital, and that if the outlook is sufficiently favorable and the economic need great enough, the required subscriptions for equity capital can be developed.

Some cooperative managements have explored approaches or procedures that would help in meeting situations of this kind. In some cases, regionals have assisted affiliated local associations through temporary stock purchases or loans. Three cooperatives joined in organizing a corporation which acquires and leases or sells property to cooperatives, thus facilitating the financing of real estate assets. In other instances, the possibility of setting up separate investment corporations to purchase stock in cooperatives has been discussed. Such purchase would be designed to build net worth to a point at which conventional financing could be arranged. A related area of exploration has been the development of a discount market for equities which, at the probable rate of revolvement, would not be paid in cash for several years.

Another idea was advanced by Dr. D. B. DeLoach when discussing this problem in 1961. After pointing out that "Modern technology, when combined with its intricate costly machines and the costs of establishing markets and procedures, has created a hurdle that is usually beyond the capabilities of most groups of farmers who might want to start a processing cooperative," he suggests that cooperatives study the feasibility of greater use of collective bargaining, which requires much smaller equity investments.[8]

In summarizing the discussion in this chapter relating to the question of whether there is a need for supplementary sources of financing for farmer cooperatives, the facts to be noted are:

1. The Federal government, in recent years, has provided additional lending authorities which are designed to assist in the development of cooperatives that serve lower-income rural populations and cannot secure reasonable credit from other sources. The trend has been to add to these authorities from time to time. There is little basis for forecasting whether, or how, the availability of government credit to farmer or rural cooperatives may be further enlarged. In any event, it may be concluded that the needs for this type of supplementary capital are being, or will be, met.

2. There is greater doubt regarding the desirability and probability of the government's providing a sizable fund from which low-interest loans could be made to finance large expansion programs that would not be attractive to conventional lenders or might be beyond their capacity. The majority of farmer cooperative leaders are strongly opposed to such a government lending program and, on balance, it would appear that the potential risks outweigh the possible benefits, particularly the benefits to farmer producers but also those to consumers. Further studies now under way, which were referred to earlier in this chapter, may throw a different light on such a conclusion.

3. There are also divergent views as to whether there is a need for some new special source of equity capital for farmer cooperatives. There is little doubt that the development and maintenance of adequate amounts of net worth represent the most difficult and most important phase in financing the growth of farmer cooperatives. For the most part, these requirements have been met, and financing generally has not been a major limitation on expansion and development. The more common view is that cooperatives and their managements can and should work out solutions for themselves. In doing so, they may utilize available assistance and counseling from the banks for cooperatives and other sources. Since, however, there is uncertainty regarding the ability of farmers and their cooperatives to generate equity capital in the amounts needed for the most effective development, a suggestion as to a supplementary source is made in Chapter Eight.

---

[8] "Growth of Farmer Cooperatives—Obstacles and Opportunities," *Journal of Farm Economics,* May 1962, pp. 489-500.

Chapter EIGHT

The Financing Job: Present and Future

In the early chapters of this book, the capital and financing needs of farmer cooperatives were first reviewed. Then the available sources of capital and the practices and problems involved in such financing (particularly those of the banks for cooperatives) were considered. Attention was given also to the adequacy of present capital sources. The final chapter will summarize some of the major facts and ideas and will examine a few selected trends to see what implications they may have regarding future financing needs and the arrangements for meeting such needs.

Cooperative Financing Now Well Developed

One of the first points to be noted is that the financing problems with which this book is concerned involve business organizations which, for the most part, have attained a relatively advanced stage of maturity. After roughly a century of trial-and-error experience, farmer cooperatives have entered a stage of business development substantially comparable to that of most other business concerns. It is of course recognized that as in virtually every other class of business organizations, there are wide variations among individual cooperatives in size, management capability, level of technological sophistication, flexibility in adjusting to change, and status as a credit risk. On the average, however, cooperatives compare favorably with the general run of responsible business concerns.

As farmer cooperatives progressed and demonstrated that they were acceptable investment and credit risks, sources and methods of financing were developed to serve their capital needs. Problems in raising needed capital thus have become less acute, and there is even competition among lenders for many cooperative loans.

Thus the cooperatives are not faced with an emergency situation in which financing is a major problem and growth and development are seriously handicapped because of inadequate capital resources. On the contrary, the financing problems involved are of the type that confront established organizations, operating and seeking to grow in a modern, dynamic, and competitive environment. Hence, important criteria in any evaluation of the financing facilities and arrangements are whether the capital supplies, the financing policies and practices, and the structure and size of the financing facilities themselves are adequate to meet the expanding requirements of the cooperatives on a business basis. If they are not adequate, ways should be explored in which they can be improved.

Some Key Summary Points

Before directing attention to questions that merit special emphasis, a brief review of some of the basic considerations in financing farmer cooperatives which have been developed in the preceding chapters may be helpful.

1. As in the case of most types of businesses, successful financing of farmer cooperatives usually requires a foundation of net worth or equity capital, but earnings may be increased and growth accelerated through the use of borrowed funds. The best combination of borrowed funds and equity capital for a cooperative varies according to the type of operation and other factors. Success stories can be cited for a variety of financial structures, ranging from virtually complete reliance on borrowed funds to the opposite extreme of nearly full dependence upon equity capital with little or no borrowings. Although variations are warranted by different sets of circumstances, a rough rule of thumb applicable to most business concerns—including most farmer cooperatives—is that borrowed funds should not exceed the amount of equity capital in the business.

2. For farmer cooperatives as a class, the major sources of equity capital, in order of importance, are: some form of retained earnings or deductions from sales, the sale of equities to members of the cooperative for cash, and sale of equities to nonmembers. In actual practice, there are wide variations in the methods of building net worth followed by individual associations. No particular type of net worth structure has been found to be uniformly successful or universally applicable to all cooperatives. There

are three important considerations which vary according to the situation: the amount of equity capital required, in view of the nature of the operations and other factors; the net worth structure, including the relative amounts of permanent and revolving capital; and the methods of net worth accumulation. These problems call for competent financial planning, and many cooperatives could benefit from the advice of experienced consultants when preparing their financial plans.

3. Excluding CCC loans, more than half of the borrowed funds used by farmer cooperatives are furnished by the banks for cooperatives. Commercial banks, the only other kind of professional lender which provides a substantial share of such credit, furnish between 10 and 20 percent of the borrowed funds, according to available figures. Members and individuals apparently exceed commercial banks as a source of credit, except for short-term, seasonal financing. There is some borrowing among cooperatives. The Federal government, of course, has been the dominant source of credit for electric and telephone cooperatives, but its financing of marketing, purchasing, and business service cooperatives is limited generally to those unable to obtain financing on a reasonable basis from other sources.

4. The relationship between the banks for cooperatives and the marketing, purchasing, and business service cooperatives includes the following: (a) as stated above, the banks are the major source of borrowed funds for the cooperatives; (b) they were created specifically to finance farmer cooperatives and, after thirty-two years of experience, they have become seasoned specialists in such financing; (c) farmer cooperatives own most of the stock in the banks and in a few years will own all of it; (d) the banks for cooperatives do not depend upon Congressional appropriations for loan funds but obtain such funds in amounts needed and at minimum cost through sale of their debentures in the general money market; (e) their capital structure has been planned so that, even after all government capital has been retired, it will be adequate to support the amounts of debenture issues necessary to meet the credit needs of farmer cooperatives in the foreseeable future; (f) the interest rates charged on loans to cooperatives generally are competitive with the rates of other professional lenders, and the net cost to borrowers will be even lower as patronage refunds are revolved and paid in cash; (g) in view of their long, specialized experience and the accompanying development of seasoned judgment, the personnel of the banks for cooperatives include individuals who are competent not only to advise on financial planning and management, but also to give counsel on many other problems that constantly confront boards of directors and managers of cooperatives.

152

5. The decision-making process in setting up a lending program for a cooperative involves: (a) recognition of statutory, regulatory, and general policy limitations and guidelines, (b) assembly of pertinent financial, operating, economic, and personnel information, and (c) evaluation of the information and of factors which are likely to affect the success or failure of the operation and the cooperative's capacity to repay the loan. Formulas or operating and financial ratios enter into the decision-making process only as part of the information collected to throw light on past performance and on the association's current and projected financial position. A study of the extensive data accumulated in the files of the banks for cooperatives confirms the long-established importance of capable management as a major factor affecting the success of the cooperative's financing as well as its overall operating results. Other decisive factors, also well-documented, are: economic need, including the necessity of adapting services and operations to changing markets and to other economic factors; a membership willing to support the cooperative with adequate business volume and investment; and an effective program for maintaining or building an appropriate net worth structure, including required working capital.

6. The equity and credit capital sources which have been developed, and the related financial management policies and plans, thus far have supported a substantial rate of growth by farmer cooperatives as a whole. While there are differences of opinion on the subject, there is little evidence to indicate that cooperative growth is being slowed down significantly by either an inadequate credit supply or restrictive credit policies. Although the net-worth phase of cooperative financing presents many difficulties, an opinion sampling indicates that very few cooperative leaders believe that the banks for cooperatives should relax their requirements in this respect or that liberal or low-interest lending by the Federal government should be expanded substantially beyond present authorities. Whatever doubts there may be about the adequacies of present financing arrangements have to do more with net worth problems than with the credit supply. This point of view, of course, does not preclude making improvements in the present credit arrangements whenever possible.

Cooperative Trends Will Affect Financing Job

As for the nature of financing requirements in the years ahead, one of the first considerations must be the direction and pattern of prospective cooperative development. Where are farmer cooperatives going? What will be the nature and rate of their growth? How will such trends affect the job of financing?

The analysis and discussion in preceding chapters indicate that many important changes and trends are now in sight which may affect future cooperative development and capital requirements. These trends include: (a) decline in the total number of farms, but an increase in the number having a profitable volume of business; (b) regional shifts of agricultural production patterns arising from changes in technology, transportation methods and costs, specialization on farms, and similar developments; (c) urbanization of farming areas; (d) widespread expansion of services and facilities throughout the business community, both vertically and horizontally, through consolidations, mergers, acquisitions, and construction; (e) technological advances that affect manufacturing methods, create new products, and modify consumer demands; (f) expansion, contraction, and other changes in foreign markets; (g) an increase in the size of business transactions, including the size of individual businesses as well as the total dollar value of all transactions and capital in use.

The foregoing changes are already under way and are likely to continue their impact upon farmer cooperative development into the indefinite future. One other factor which may have considerable effect upon the ultimate role of cooperatives is the probable long-range tapering-off of farm programs requiring public funds, which will necessitate greater reliance by farmers on self-help solutions to their economic problems. The potential place of cooperatives in such self-help efforts has been pointed out, but may be further illustrated by one of the recommendations made by the National Agricultural Advisory Commission in its report *Farm Policy In The Years Ahead*. Recommendation 18 states in part:

> Both the opportunities for and the necessity of cooperative action by farmers to assert themselves in the markets in which they deal will increase in the future. A greater proportion of the responsibility for maintaining fair and stable incomes in agriculture can be shifted, selectively and gradually, from strictly government programs to producers' own efforts as the change occurs. It should be part of our national farm policy to expedite sound developments of this kind in every reasonable way. A new and growing role for farmers' cooperatives, together with more participation by producers in marketing their own products, will necessarily be an important part of the total change. It will also be essential to preserve a competitive environment in the processing and distribution industries such that producers have a fair chance to compete on even terms.[1]

Policies and attitudes toward farm problems and farmer cooperatives vary with changing administrations. In recent years there has been significant interest by the Federal government in implementing the role of cooperatives suggested in the recommendation quoted above. Shortly

---

[1] U. S. Department of Agriculture, November 1964, p. 37.

after his appointment, Secretary of Agriculture Orville Freeman designated a National Advisory Committee on Cooperatives to make recommendations regarding the role that cooperatives might play in improving American agriculture and to suggest steps that could be taken toward that end. One of the first steps was the National Conference on Cooperatives and the Future, held in Washington, D. C., on April 28, 1963. Later, the department set up a task force to examine more intensively the questions raised during the conference, particularly from the standpoint of the part which the department might play and the implementing legislation which might be needed. Congress also has provided additional credit and other assistance designed to encourage development of cooperatives in the lower-income farming areas. Through speeches and statements, high officers of the Department of Agriculture, and even the President, have supported the potential role that farmer cooperatives might play. Still another step taken by the department was the designation of October 1964 as Cooperative Month.

These trends in attitudes and economic circumstances indicate that farmer cooperatives can play an increasingly important part in the agricultural industries of the United States if they are able to adapt successfully to the changing economic, technological and competitive conditions. During an address to the National Marketing Service Workshop in November 1964, J. K. Samuels, director of the Marketing Division of the Farmer Cooperative Service, enumerated the following steps which he believes farmer cooperatives must take if they are to make the required adjustments effectively and meet the challenge to play a more important role:

1. There is need for better management. This means following sound principles of management and finance. It means clearly defined duties of the board of directors and the manager. It means that cooperatives will have to give more attention to management training because management skills are in short supply.

2. Cooperatives must learn to cooperate together, especially in areas of joint sales, joint promotional and advertising efforts, and coordinated marketing programs.

3. Cooperatives should seek out opportunities for new services to members both in marketing and in production supplies essential to farming.

4. Cooperatives must become larger and stronger. Only 5 cooperatives are among the 500 largest U. S. industrial corporations listed by *Fortune* (July 1963).[2] Only 100 cooperatives have a volume of busi-

---

[2] The July 1964 issue of *Fortune* indicated that the number of cooperatives in the largest 500 corporations had increased to 6.

ness of over $20 million annually. On the other hand, over 73 percent of the marketing and purchasing cooperatives have a volume of business of less than $1 million. Cooperatives can grow internally by merging or consolidating with other cooperatives and by acquiring other businesses. We see much evidence of this growth among cooperatives today.

5. Cooperatives need to become more diversified. By diversification they can spread their risks, can tap wider sources of financing because they will be better credit risks, can employ better management, and can merchandise their products to better advantage.

6. Cooperatives need to establish strict membership requirements, particularly as they relate to product quality. To meet the ever-increasing demands of the market for uniform products of good quality, many cooperatives will need to confine their membership to growers who can produce a top-quality product. The cooperative cannot, any more than any other marketing agency, continue to sell successfully a heterogeneous supply offered by farmers.

7. Cooperatives will have to assume more control over production of commodities they market. Cooperatives more and more will have to set quality standards for raw products, prescribe production practices and then see to it that their farmer members live up to such requirements. This gives the farmer advantages both in efficiency and quality.

8. Many cooperatives in the future, as in the past, will have to start small or begin with a limited service to their members. There is still a place in the marketing picture for the small cooperative that can provide an efficient assembly, packing, and grading job in the local community. However, more and more it will be necessary for such local associations to join together or tie in with larger cooperatives for selling, merchandising, and purchasing supplies.

Although the foregoing statements were addressed to a cooperative marketing audience, most of the eight points have equal application to supply and business service associations. The ideas are also consistent with those expressed by the cooperative leaders interviewed in the earlier study made by the author for the banks for cooperatives.

Cooperatives already have gone far in the directions outlined. Their success in achieving further progress will depend mainly on the alertness, aggressiveness, and wisdom of the managers and directors of individual associations and of cooperative leaders in general. But adequate and intelligent financing also will be necessary. Although the elements of effective financing programs have already been discussed, a few points are worthy of additional emphasis.

Equity Capital Requirements

Throughout this book, and in interviews with cooperative leaders, the basic role of equity capital or net worth in any financing program has been stressed. Some of the major issues relating to net worth which have been discussed are: the necessity for an adequate foundation or cushion of net worth; sources or methods of building net worth; the amount of net worth which will both assure effective financial management and satisfy lenders' requirements; and alternative policies regarding the management or the composition of the net-worth structure.

Considerations in resolving these questions need not be repeated, but two points should be re-emphasized. The first is that each cooperative must develop an individual program which will be geared to its all-important financial plan. The association management must have well-thought-out ideas about where the cooperative is going and how it will get there. The other point is that, in developing this plan, many cooperatives obtain help from consultants or financing specialists. Officers and staff members of the banks for cooperatives, with their extensive experience in financing cooperatives, are one of the most important sources of counseling assistance in financial management.

One major issue merits further attention. It is the question of whether the overall rate of net-worth accumulation is adequate to support the growth and development needed by cooperatives in order to hold and improve their competitive position. Available statistics are for the most part encouraging, but they do not provide a firm answer.

Most cooperative leaders believe that this problem is being handled well and will be resolved successfully. It is their opinion that if efficient management, tangible savings and benefits to patrons, and an effective educational program are evident, members will not hesitate to provide the investments in equity capital needed for operations and reasonable growth. This view is supported by the analysis of the lending experience of the banks for cooperatives which was summarized in Chapter Three.

Nevertheless, the difficulties must be recognized. Some facts are not encouraging, and differences of opinion exist as to solutions. It is possible that conditions might develop which would justify the establishment of special sources of equity capital. Some Federal government assistance might be appropriate and acceptable, particularly if legislation should shift the emphasis in agricultural programs toward self-help efforts in which cooperatives would play a prominent role.

A plan, therefore, is herein proposed for consideration in the event that some special measure should appear justified. In designing this proposal, the author has tried to benefit from previous experiences of the Federal government in providing financial aid to cooperatives and has incorporated ideas which have been used successfully in the past and would require a minimum of government funds and intervention. The following outline of this plan gives only the main features and some of the reasoning behind them. Many details, of course, would have to be worked out.

Plan for Providing Supplementary Equity Capital

A corporation would be established for the purpose of purchasing preferred stock in farmer cooperatives. Such purchases would be made only in cases where all other circumstances were favorable and a bank for cooperatives was willing to provide needed credit if additional equity capital could be raised. The corporation would subscribe to preferred stock only in situations where for some good reason the amount of risk capital required as an appropriate basis for credit could not be obtained from members or other sources.

The capital of the corporation would be subscribed by the Federal government from the banks for cooperatives revolving fund and by farmer cooperatives in amounts or ratios to be determined. The preferred stock subscribed in cooperatives would carry a moderate rate of cumulative dividend with provision for eventual retirement. In servicing its loan, the bank for cooperatives also would automatically service the corporation's investment and keep the corporation informed of the progress of the cooperative. Preferably, the corporation should be administered within the Farm Credit System, under the guidance of a board of directors, in order to facilitate close working relationships with the lending banks for cooperatives.

There are several reasons for proposing the type of approach sketched above. In the first place, it would provide equity capital rather than credit, because of the prevalent belief that if there is a financing gap or handicap to growth it is mainly in the equity capital area. Credit supplies are ample, and therefore no new credit facilities are needed. Capital stock would be subscribed in a cooperative only after thorough investigation had convinced the corporation that all means of raising member capital had been exhausted. When the gap in equity capital had been filled by the corporation's subscription, the way would be opened for credit financing by a bank for cooperatives.

A second point is that the government capital which would be used would come from the revolving fund that was originally established by Congress to finance farmer cooperatives and is still earmarked for possible further use in such development. This proposed use of a part of the fund

158

is consistent with the policy previously declared by Congress in the Agricultural Marketing Act of 1929. Use of money already in the revolving fund is a financing method least likely to conflict with government budgetary considerations. The successful experience of government financial help through capital stock subscriptions in the Federal Deposit Insurance Corporation, the Federal Home Loan Banks and the Farm Credit System would be a favorable precedent.

Another important feature of the plan is that the administration would be within the Farm Credit System, where there is a great accumulation of know-how in the financing of farmer cooperatives and where appropriate working relationships with the banks for cooperatives could be maintained. It may be noted also that this proposal borrows some features from the former production credit corporations which subscribed to stock in the production credit associations, and that it has some features of the small business investment corporations in which capital is subscribed by both government and private business and which, in turn, may make investments in equity capital of small business concerns.

While the author believes that an investment corporation such as that suggested would be workable, practical, and politically acceptable, it should be re-emphasized that it is proposed only as an emergency measure. Although there may be difficulties, experience has indicated that if farmers are convinced of the need and have confidence in the leadership, they will continue to provide the foundation capital required by their cooperatives for effective operation and growth. However, if the outlook has been misjudged or emergency conditions should develop, the author believes that it would be advantageous to both the cooperatives and the public to develop additional capital for farmer cooperatives by supplementing equity capital sources rather than by increasing government loan funds.

Adapting Credit Facilities to Change

The ideas expressed in the preceding discussions of equity capital reflect the broad viewpoint that although farmer cooperatives may be at some disadvantage in not being able to market equity interests that have capital gains potential, they have a definite advantage in the credit sources available to them. Credit services to farmer cooperatives are well developed, and the indications are that they will be ample for future needs.

With respect to the potential credit supply, several facts should be noted. Under the processes referred to in the beginning of Chapter Two, this nation leads the world in capital formation and resources. Commercial banks and other financial intermediaries are able to channel available capital and credit to acceptable users. The Federal Reserve System is designed to provide flexibility in the credit flow so that the supply can be readily adjusted to overall needs. Except for the times when credit is deliberately restricted in order to check overexpansion, the total capital and credit supply in the United States is ample not only to meet the sound domestic needs but also to provide sizable investments abroad.

This credit supply is available to farmer cooperatives. They have access to it through the intermediaries used also by their competing agribusinesses, especially through commercial banks. In addition the cooperatives have a banking system created specifically for their use, which they will own completely in a few years. To some degree, in fact, farmer cooperatives can now negotiate with lenders for the best credit terms.

Cooperative leaders and managements should consider their policies in this regard, especially the long-term implications, very carefully. In the first place, they should not underestimate or overlook the very substantial contributions made by the banks for cooperatives in the attainment of the present stage of development by farmer cooperatives. At the time the banks began operations, the agricultural industry was struggling to establish financial solvency after several years of severe depression. Furthermore, farmer cooperatives in general were not regarded as desirable credit risks by most conventional lenders.

In these circumstances, the banks for cooperatives not only made loans when credit was not otherwise available, but also worked with other agencies in providing greatly needed counseling on organization and operating problems, especially on financial management. As cooperatives grew and developed strength, demonstrating the effectiveness of these credit and counseling services, the way was shown to other lenders. Wider sources of credit thus were opened up to cooperatives, leading gradually to the present favorable situation. While other influences must be recognized, there is little doubt that the services of the banks for cooperatives were an extremely important factor in this development.

In the second place, cooperative managements should give serious thought to future borrowing policies and their possible impact upon the present favorable credit supply. How consistently should they support, with their patronage, their own credit organizations, even if occasionally they might be able to negotiate more advantageous terms with other lenders? What would be the long-term impact upon the effectiveness of the banks for cooperatives of an extensive shift of patronage to other lenders? Could the present favorable position with respect to credit supply and related services be maintained?

The steady growth of the loan volume and financial strength of the banks for cooperatives indicates strong support with respect to both patronage and investment. There is no evidence of any incipient reversal of this trend. Most cooperative leaders are aware that the banks need a continual growth in loan volume in order to attract and hold competent officers and staff and to operate at maximum efficiency.

The banks for cooperatives, in turn, must maintain the high quality and effectiveness of their services in order to merit the support of cooperatives. Basically, such service involves the same factors that contribute to the successful growth of cooperatives, and were described in Chapter Three during the analysis of the banks' extensive lending experience. The policies essential to such success receive close attention from the banks' boards of directors and their supervising organization, the Farm Credit Administration.

As a final point in considering the task of financing farmer cooperatives in the future, one of the basic factors referred to above merits re-emphasis. That is the necessity, in a fast-moving, dynamic society, of keeping alert to changes in financing needs of farmer cooperatives and of making necessary and appropriate adjustments in policies and services.

In most respects, the banks for cooperatives have built-in flexibility which will permit adjustment to these changing requirements. They have the capacity to expand credit volume in whatever amounts can be reasonably anticipated to be necessary for the foreseeable future. The banks' experience since beginning the issuance of consolidated debentures has shown that the debentures have a sufficiently dependable market so that they can be sold in the required amounts even during difficult market situations and business recessions such as those experienced after World War II. While market conditions affect the rates of interest which must be paid, there has been no problem in obtaining the amounts of loanable funds needed. Furthermore, as has been pointed out, when all government capital has been repaid by the banks for cooperatives and member capital is revolved, the cash distributions from margins will have the effect of reducing the net cost of credit to borrowers.

The present net worth of the banks, together with the available revolving fund, will support more than $3 billion of loans. Since the outstanding total is in the vicinity of $1 billion, the banks have the capacity to finance cooperative growth for many years to come. The potential loan demands are under almost continuous study as part of the financial planning by the banks. The amounts of net worth can be adapted to the needs by adjusting the rate of cash investment of Class C stock and the rate of revolving Class C stock.

Another aspect of the banks' operations which may require adjustment to changing needs and conditions involves the non-lending services. The counseling and leadership activities are extremely important and obviously must be geared to current developments, to the wishes of the borrower-owners, and to the best interests of farmer cooperatives in general.

In Chapter Five, it was suggested that certain restrictions on term loans established by law be removed. Thus far, these limitations have not seriously handicapped the banks in tailoring their lending programs to meet the individual needs. As cooperatives increase in size, complexity, and financial responsibility, and as the inevitable new problems arise, rules that were established a third of a century ago are likely to become a handicap. It was further suggested in Chapter Five that if the legal restrictions were removed, the controls or regulations that might be needed should become the responsibility of the supervisory body, the Farm Credit Administration. This agency not only is in a position to know what regulations are appropriate, but also would be able to make changes much more quickly, if and when they were needed, than is usually possible through the more time-consuming legislative route. Regulations of the Farm Credit Administration normally are worked out in consultation with the banks' officers and directors. In this manner, lending policies are coordinated throughout the system and are updated to meet the changing needs of borrowers.

As farmer cooperatives increase in complexity and overall size, and especially in amounts invested in fixed assets, there may be increased interest in putting part of their financing on a long-term basis comparable to long-term bonds used by some corporations. Certain cooperatives already have experimented with bond issues. Some long-term financing also has been obtained from other sources, such as life insurance companies. The costs, dependability, and other aspects of such financing should be carefully compared with the term financing available to cooperatives through their own banking system. While circumstances may change, the present prospect is that relatively small bond issues by individual cooperatives are likely to cost more than term financing from the banks for cooperatives, which obtain funds at wholesale "agency" rates and adjust the rates on term loans to changes in the cost of money. The latter arrangement also provides greater flexibility, since the term loans and other financing can be reshaped as frequently as growth requires, without the expense of new bond issues. In addition, any comparisons of alternative methods of financing should take account of the situation which will exist when the banks for cooperatives begin to revolve their Class C stock.

The banks for cooperatives, for their part, must keep alert to any changes in money market conditions and in the needs of cooperatives in order to keep their services updated. For example, the relative merits of issuing a part of their debentures for longer terms, so that they would be parallel

162

to the longer-term loans made, have been studied from time to time. The conclusions thus far have been that the best procedure under recent money market conditions has been to offer only debentures with relatively short terms, usually of six months or less. This policy can quickly be changed, if necessary, to adjust to any important modification in the structure of market rates of interest.

Furthermore, the thirty-seven Farm Credit banks, as a group, have studied the entire process of obtaining loan funds. The procedure which has been in use for many years has been compared with other possible methods of obtaining funds, including sale of securities by competitive bidding, negotiated prices and private placement, the use of commercial paper, savings deposits, local sales, and methods used by other government agencies. All such studies showed either that the present procedure resulted in funds being obtained at lower costs or that there would be no real advantage in changing. Here again, the Farm Credit banks should keep alert to any significant developments which might warrant some modification in the method of obtaining loan funds. At present, however, the banks for cooperatives have a method of marketing their debentures which is well adapted to conditions now in sight and which will meet the need for loan funds efficiently and dependably.

Another area of potential adjustment for both banks and cooperatives stems from a combination of changes frequently referred to as the urbanization of agriculture. A number of problems with financing implications may be created by the spread of the nonfarming population into rural areas and the resultant new relationship between farmer-producers and nonfarm consumers. The shift in population is shown in Figure 5 which projects the employment status of the rural population for the year 1970.

One aspect of this population shift is that some activities or problems which were formerly included in "farm" categories are now referred to as "rural" in order to acknowledge the change in the character of the countryside. Most of the new members of electric cooperatives are nonfarming rural residents. The authorities to lend to cooperatives provided by the Area Redevelopment Act of 1961 and the Economic Opportunity Act of 1964 permit loans to rural cooperatives rather than to farmer cooperatives. There have even been proposals to change the name of the United States Department of Agriculture to reflect in some way its responsibilities to a broadened rural population.

Farmer supply cooperatives in a number of areas have an interest in these trends. As farm land is taken up by suburban and industrial development and the number of farmers is further reduced by changes in the size and nature of farm operations, the potential number of farmer-members of cooperatives declines. Supply cooperatives are considering

163

how far they should go in encouraging patronage from nonfarm rural residents and, especially, the extent to which nonfarm patrons should be admitted to membership. This latter question is important because of the requirement that a cooperative is eligible to borrow from a bank for cooperatives only if 90 percent of the voting media is held by producers or by cooperatives eligible to borrow from the banks.

Most farmer cooperatives, especially the marketing cooperatives, have resisted efforts to lower the eligibility requirement because of the fear that it might eventually lead to loss of farmer control of the cooperatives. As urbanization progresses, however, such efforts will undoubtedly continue. It is possible that if the 90 percent requirement is not modified, more cooperatives may seek financing from commercial banks or under Federal government authorities where no similar eligibility requirement is a factor.

The problem just stated is of greatest concern to farmer supply cooperatives, and possibly to some marketing cooperatives that have also developed extensive supply services. Marketing cooperatives are also exploring relations with nonfarm consumers, but from a different point of view. Their incentive in such exploration is in finding ways to improve their image with consumers in order to broaden or stabilize the market for their products. With these objectives in mind, some groups have studied the possibility of acquiring control of retail outlets. If such control were obtained through purchase, the financing needs might be very large.

Another approach to the problem of developing retail outlets for farmer marketing cooperatives is to establish working relationships with consumer cooperatives. One such effort, probably still in the experimental stage, is a cooperative which is owned equally by a farmer-producer cooperative on the one hand and a consumer cooperative and other retail establishments on the other. The association performs intermediate services between the producer and the retailer, and divides any savings between the two groups of stockholders. This arrangement is designed to bridge the gap between farmer producers and consumers. If past history is any guide, it seems unlikely that consumer cooperatives will grow large enough to offer an outlet for a substantial share of the products of farmer cooperatives.

Time alone will reveal the ways in which farmer cooperatives adapt their supply services to the increasing number of rural nonfarm consumers and the routes they follow in seeking to stabilize or control general consumer markets for their products. Each possibility would have different financing implications. Extensive investment in retail outlets, for example, would present greater financing problems than emphasis on collective bargaining. Also, some policies might affect the cooperatives' eligibility to borrow from the banks for cooperatives under present requirements. In that event, the pressure for change might be increased. In addition, tax and other considerations might be involved.

Other changes now in sight which have financing implications have been discussed. Still others, not now foreseen, may develop. But with capable and imaginative leadership, seasoned by extensive financing experience, there is little doubt that the banks for cooperatives, supplemented by other capital and credit sources, will make whatever adaptations are necessary to meet the changing credit requirements of farmer cooperatives throughout the United States.

Concluding Observations

As determined by this study, major considerations in evaluating the financing and credit resources available to farmer cooperatives in the United States may be summarized as follows:

1. Financing sources and facilities are well-developed and, for the most part, sufficient for the legitimate credit needs of farmer cooperatives.

2. To the limited extent that cooperative development and growth may have been retarded because of financing difficulties, the deficiency in recent years has been mainly in equity capital rather than credit. This conclusion recognizes that sound financing permits considerable variation in the proportions of owned and borrowed capital, depending upon the kind of operation and other factors.

3. Effective methods of net-worth accumulation have been developed by many successful cooperatives. Although adequate net worth, by itself, is not a guarantee of success, many other cooperatives could benefit by adapting such proven methods to their particular situations. However, as conditions change, even the tested procedures may require modification. Hence, net worth structures and sources should be studied continuously by individual cooperatives, research agencies, and lenders, particularly the banks for cooperatives. It is conceivable that such further study might show that the establishment of some additional or supplementary source of equity capital would be justified.

4. For the foreseeable future, credit supplies are ample. Cooperatives that are able to meet statutory and other requirements of the banks for cooperatives and commercial banks can obtain from these sources all of the borrowed capital necessary for successful operation and growth. Federal government credit is becoming available in increasing amounts for those unable to meet these qualifications. Members of cooperatives,

manufacturers, and other suppliers round out the total credit supply. The evidence reveals no significant demand or need for new credit facilities. For borrowing cooperatives, the problems in this area consist chiefly of maintaining credit worthiness through efficient operation and good financial management; for lenders, they consist of keeping lending policies and procedures up to date.

5. Since the banks for cooperatives provide more than half of the credit used by farmer cooperatives and will soon be completely owned by borrower-cooperatives, these banks received major attention in this book. The evidence shows that their lending and counseling services have contributed extensively and effectively to the development and growth of farmer cooperatives in the United States. As a banking system, they are successfully doing the job for which they were created.

6. Along with these accomplishments, there have inevitably been some human mistakes and some dissatisfaction and criticism. The author had full freedom to ferret out, examine, and evaluate objectively many such incidents and the related facts. It was noted that criticism or dissatisfaction frequently stemmed from differences of opinion regarding decisions on individual loans. Occasionally, it appeared that sweeping generalizations regarding loan policies were based on one or two controversial actions. In some cases, criticisms arose from incomplete or inaccurate information.

The investigation revealed no need of, or widespread demand for, any major revamping of lending policies or methods of operation. Numerous changes, both legislative and regulatory, have been made since the banks were organized in 1933. Such modifications have improved their organization and procedures and have helped them to adjust their services to the changing needs of cooperatives and to the environment in which the banks and their borrowers operate.

Consideration of such adjustments and innovations are continuously necessary in a dynamic economy. The managements of the banks for cooperatives and the supervisory staff of the Farm Credit Administration have open minds toward new ideas. A review of bank conference agendas indicated that proposals of various kinds were under constant study. Some suggestions for changes in legislation and other areas which the author believes would assist the banks in improving or updating services have been made in this book.

7. Basically, the factors which are likely to assure the continued effectiveness of the banks for cooperatives are the same as those which are essential to the success of farmer cooperatives. Factors of special importance to the banks include experienced and well-trained officers and

other personnel, capable boards of directors, loyal and well-informed member patrons, and vigilant and able leadership by the Washington supervisory staff.

Finally, it should be stressed that the great majority of individual cooperatives and their regional and national organizations are to be commended for their past interest and patronage, as evidenced by the rapid progress toward complete farmer cooperative ownership of the banks through the retirement of government capital. The level of such support, and the future attention given by cooperative leadership to the banks' affairs will be influential in determining the extent to which the full benefits of a cooperatively-owned financing system are realized.

The Banks for Cooperatives

As long as a supply is available, copies of this book may be obtained from any of the banks for cooperatives, which are:

Springfield Bank for Cooperatives
310 State Street
Springfield, Massachusetts 01101

St. Paul Bank for Cooperatives
346 Jackson Street
St. Paul, Minnesota 55101

Baltimore Bank for Cooperatives
St. Paul and 24th Streets
Baltimore, Maryland 21203

Omaha Bank for Cooperatives
206 South 19th Street
Omaha, Nebraska 68102

Columbia Bank for Cooperatives
1401 Hampton Street
Columbia, South Carolina 29202

Wichita Bank for Cooperatives
Douglas Avenue and Main Street
Wichita, Kansas 67202

Louisville Bank for Cooperatives
224 East Broadway
Louisville, Kentucky 40202

Houston Bank for Cooperatives
430 Lamar Avenue
Houston, Texas 77001

New Orleans Bank for Cooperatives
860 St. Charles Avenue
New Orleans, Louisiana 70150

Berkeley Bank for Cooperatives
2180 Milvia Street
Berkeley, California 94701

St. Louis Bank for Cooperatives
506 Olive Street
St. Louis, Missouri 63166

Spokane Bank for Cooperatives
North 214 Wall Street
Spokane, Washington 99201

Central Bank for Cooperatives
425 13th Street, N.W.
Washington, D. C. 20044

Copies also may be obtained from:

Cooperative Bank Service
Farm Credit Administration
Washington, D. C. 20578